The Cozy Table

THE
Cozy Table

100 Recipes for One, Two, or a Few

DANA DeVOLK

THE COUNTRYMAN PRESS
A division of W. W. Norton & Company
Independent Publishers Since 1923

To Jeremy,
my #1 fan and
favorite taste tester

CONTENTS

Introduction

For me, food is life. In a sense, food is life for all of us—we have to eat to survive. But, for me, it is a passion. My biggest passion. I go to bed every night with thoughts of a new recipe or how to tweak a certain baking technique. I always wake up ready to get in the kitchen to start my day, while also kicking myself for not writing down said new recipe or baking technique. Will I ever learn?

I grew up a northern southerner. Yes, I'm just as confused as you are. Half of my childhood was spent in the Chicago suburbs and the other half smack in the middle of North Carolina. I have a passion for foods from both the North and South, which you will find throughout this cookbook.

My love of food started at a young age. And that love ultimately bloomed into my career. When I was little, I knew what I wanted to be . . . a CHEF! After graduating from high school, I got my culinary arts degree and achieved my dream of becoming that chef! I worked in professional kitchens until starting my blog, *This Silly Girl's Kitchen*, in 2012 and it is now my full-time job.

On my blog, I love teaching my readers tips and tricks I learned from the restaurant industry and I incorporate them into my recipes. Through-out this book I have added "pro tips": little nuggets of information about why I use certain techniques. Trust me on this: I've got your back!

Family is another passion of mine. I have amazing memories of growing up surrounded by my cousins and just having a blast. For me, they are more like siblings since, as an only child, I really got attached to them. One of my favorite childhood memories is of a huge group of us going down to the beach and my southern grandma making all of us kids tomato sandwiches loaded with mayonnaise on simple white bread. Even now, every time I step out of my back door on summer mornings here in Florida, I can smell and feel that special trip in the air and taste those vine-ripe tomatoes.

That is what food does to us. It triggers memories and immediately we can be transferred back in time. That is exactly the feeling I tried to encapsulate here. Make my Spaghetti and Meatballs with Sausage (page 39) and you will go straight to my mother's kitchen and see me in the corner sneaking a meatball after school. Chicago-Style Deep Dish Pizza (page 36)? That's all my dad's doing. Strawberry Shortcakes (page 137), and I remember the first time I ever tasted the real deal, thanks to my northern grandma. But I cannot tell you how many recipes in this book remind me of my southern grandma, whose biggest wish was just to have family around and serve us a humungous meal. I truly would not be writing these words today without her.

What does all this have to do with *The Cozy Table*, you might ask? Cozy = comfort. Comfort food has always been my favorite way to cook. Mixing together tried-and-true family recipes and putting twists on them to make it my own. I love to elevate classic dishes and tweak them into something new and exciting. This whole book is just one big ball of love wrapped in comfort. Comfort food, a hug from those you love put onto a plate, just waiting to be devoured. There is positively no food better than comfort food. But one thing that I have come across in my years of cooking is . . . comfort food is normally made for a crowd. Most likely you will see multiple-portion recipes for soups and sauces, seven-layer cakes, and enough broccoli rice casserole to feed an army! In this cookbook, things are laid out a little differently. I pare down those large comfort food recipes to be accessible to feed one, two, or a few people at a time. This book is perfect for anyone from newlyweds to empty nesters!

I have tested these recipes over and over so they come out right each time. Now, with this book, I have opened up my personal kitchen to you, handing over the recipes I make every week. I truly hope you and your family enjoy them and start to make some more memories of your own, tucked in around your cozy table!

How to Use This Book

I highly suggest that before making any recipe in this book, you read the entire recipe through first. I have included notes and pro tips throughout, and to get a good idea of what you will need to execute the recipe successfully, these also need to be read through. When I first started cooking, I ran into a lot of mistakes by not doing this. By reading the recipe through, you will know whether you need to preheat the oven right away or if preheating can wait until those potatoes are cooked. You will also know which ingredients need to be on hand and ready to use, so you won't run into any surprises halfway into the recipe.

Ingredients

The ingredients used in these recipes are straightforward and you can easily find them in your local grocery store. However, please keep these tips in mind before starting!

- Vegetables used anywhere in this book should be washed thoroughly and ready to cook. Make sure, before you start each recipe, to wash your veggies first!
- All butter used in this cookbook is unsalted. That is how I always cook, and this way you always know just how much salt is going into a dish. Plus, next time you go to make those Jumbo Chocolate Chip Cookies (page 144), you will already have the right butter on hand!
- Most of the recipes in this book are 100 percent homemade. But if you find using some store-bought ingredients makes it easier, I say go for it! Except for the cream cheese crust for the Creamy Chicken Potpies (page 67) and Cheesy Bacon and Kale Quiche (page 71). You HAVE to try that crust—it's life changing.

Equipment

For small-batch recipes, some special equipment will help you make the dishes properly. Here is a list of items you will need:

- 1 (3-quart) saucepan
- 2 cast-iron or oven-safe skillets (one 6- and one 8-inch)
- 1 (5-inch) baking dish (round or square)
- 1 muffin tin
- 1 mini muffin tin
- 2 (9-inch) round cake pans
- Several mini loaf pans (about 2½ by 4 inches) or one larger loaf pan with multiple mini-loaf cavities
- Wire cooling rack
- Pizza stone (the best way to get that perfect, crispy crust, but you can use a baking sheet if you don't have one)
- Pizza peel (recommended)
- Grill (or a grill pan)
- Slow cooker
- Blender or immersion blender
- Electric mixer (stand mixer recommended but not necessary)
- 1 (4-inch) round cookie cutter
- Mesh strainer
- Zester (this is my favorite tool to "mince" garlic)
- Mandoline (very useful to have but not 100 percent necessary if you are confident in those knife skills!)

Apps 'N' Snacks

7-Layer Dip Totchos

Seven-layer dip is one of those iconic, nostalgic appetizers. Layers of beans, cheese, sour cream, and other goodies makes it a go-to dip for get-togethers! Totchos have been a fun staple for a while now, incorporating nacho toppings on Tater Tots for a yummy twist. Instead of classic nacho toppings, I mix it up with seven layers of deliciousness as a nod to childhood!

26 frozen Tater Tots, or similar product

½ cup refried beans

¼ cup diced tomato (from 1 medium tomato)

½ cup shredded sharp Cheddar (or cheese blend of your choice)

½ avocado, peeled, pitted, and mashed

¼ cup sour cream

2 tablespoons Green Salsa (page 170) or salsa of your choice

1 tablespoon roughly chopped cilantro

1 scallion, thinly sliced

Note: Included on page 170 is a recipe for an amazing green salsa using tomatillos! You can use this salsa on lots of other yummy dishes as well, such as Grilled Chicken Tacos (page 47) and Ultimate Nachos (page 27)!

1. Preheat the oven to 425°F.

2. Place the Tater Tots, in a single layer, in an 8-inch cast-iron skillet or oven-safe dish. Bake for 20 minutes.

3. Top the Tater Tots with the beans, tomato, and cheese. Bake for an additional 3 minutes, until the cheese is melted.

4. Top with the mashed avocado, sour cream, and salsa. Garnish with the cilantro and sliced scallion.

Sausage Dip Pinwheels

Two classics combine to make one creamy, slightly spicy appetizer! I love serving these on game day or at any party. They also make a great afternoon snack or even dinner alongside a salad!

4 ounces ground pork sausage

2 ounces cream cheese, softened

5 tablespoons canned diced tomatoes with green chiles, drained

½ sheet canned crescent dough (see note)

Garlic Salad Dressing (page 173), for serving (optional)

Note: Once opened, crescent dough needs to be cooked. I recommend doubling this recipe to use the full can— these pinwheels are that good!

1. Preheat the oven to 375°F.

2. Cook the sausage in a skillet until cooked through and golden brown; drain on a paper towel–lined tray. Transfer to a bowl and mix with the cream cheese and tomatoes; set aside.

3. Unroll the half-sheet of crescent dough and cover three-quarters of the dough with the sausage mixture. Roll up tightly, using the last fourth of the dough as the outside edge. Cut into eighths and place, right side up, on an ungreased cookie sheet. Bake for 11 to 13 minutes, until golden brown. Let cool slightly and serve plain or with Garlic Salad Dressing for dipping.

Variation:
Don't like spicy foods? Use a can of regular diced tomatoes instead of one with chiles.

Classic Cheeseburger Sliders

Burgers are just one of those comfort foods loved by all. I'll take them any way I can get them, but there is something about cooking out on a warm summer night that I really love. Surrounded by twinkling fireflies, a lazy breeze, and the aroma of burgers cooking over the charcoals, it doesn't get much better than that!

Living in Florida, I have the privilege of using my grill year-round. But during long winters in Chicago when I was growing up, there was no way you would be caught outside grilling! So, I made this recipe using a cast-iron skillet indoors. Perfect for sliders!

½ pound lean ground beef (93/7)
2 teaspoons Worcestershire sauce
½ teaspoon garlic powder
¼ teaspoon onion powder
¼ teaspoon Montreal steak seasoning
3 cracks black pepper
1 tablespoon unsalted butter (or leftover bacon grease if you have it)
½ medium sweet onion, diced
4 slider buns
2 slices sharp Cheddar, cut in half
Garlic Mayonnaise (page 175)
Suggested toppings: sliced Roma tomato (seasoned with salt and freshly ground black pepper), lettuce, and pickles

1. Place the ground beef, Worcestershire sauce, garlic powder, onion powder, Montreal seasoning, and black pepper in a medium bowl. Mix by hand until the spices are evenly distributed throughout the meat. Divide into four equal portions, roll each into a ball, and refrigerate until ready to cook.

2. Heat a large cast-iron skillet over medium heat until hot. Place the butter in the pan and immediately add the onion. Cook, stirring occasionally, for 5 to 8 minutes, until the onion is translucent and slightly browned. Remove the onion from the pan and set aside, reserving the pan and its cooking fat.

3. Get your toppings ready now—the burgers cook very fast and you will be serving in no time! If you like the slider buns to be toasted, do that now, too.

4. Heat the same cast-iron pan over medium heat until hot, then place the burgers in the pan, 2 to 3 inches apart. Using a flat spatula or the bottom of a clean, flat surface, such as a

Note: This is the perfectly sized recipe for two, but I recommend doubling the recipe and freezing the patties for another time.

coffee mug, flatten the patties as thinly as you can. Cook for 3 minutes. Flip, top with cheese, and cook for an additional 3 minutes.

5. Assemble the burgers as you wish with your favorite toppings, including the onion and garlic mayonnaise.

Variations:
Mix these up with your favorite cheese, bacon, and condiments.

Meatball Sub Cups

This is another fun appetizer to have for game day or any party. Cute, cheesy, and full of flavor, these Meatball Sub Cups are even great as a weeknight meal!

Cooking spray
1 sheet puff pastry
1 large egg, lightly beaten
2 tablespoons freshly grated
  Parmigiano-Reggiano
4 prepared Meatballs
  (page 39)
1 cup Spaghetti Sauce
  (page 39)
1 cup shredded provolone

Note: This is a fantastic recipe to use any leftovers from spaghetti and meatballs night! I recommend using the meat-ball recipe on page 39. But in a pinch, frozen will work, too.

1. Preheat the oven to 400°F. Turn a muffin tin upside down and spray four of the cup bases (their outside bottom) with cooking spray.

2. Roll out the puff pastry and prick all over with a fork. Using a 4-inch round cookie cutter, cut out four circles. Drop the circles over the prepared muffin cup bases. Letting the dough overlap on the sides, press each circle down slightly to form a bowl. Brush with the egg and sprinkle with the Parmesan.

3. Bake for 15 minutes, or until golden brown.

4. While the cups are baking, place the meat-balls and sauce in a pot and heat through over medium heat.

5. Take the pastry cups off the muffin tin and place, right side up, on a baking sheet. Place one meatball in the center of each cup and spoon a little sauce over it. Sprinkle ¼ cup of the provo-lone over each cup. Place back in the oven and cook for 3 minutes, until the cheese has melted.

6. Serve with the remaining sauce.

Roasted Garlic Cream Cheese Dip

This is one of those simple recipes that is just a knockout. Every month or so my husband, Jeremy, will start begging me to make him this dip. For the game, of course, but I know he just can't keep away from this addictive, creamy dip! You can't go wrong with cream cheese and roasted garlic. Alongside my Homemade Potato Chips (following page), you've got a home run of an appetizer or side dish! It would also be a wonderful spread for bagels.

8 ounces cream cheese, softened
1 head Roasted Garlic (page 174)
½ cup sour cream
2 cracks black pepper
Homemade Potato Chips (page 24), freshly cut veggies, or even store-bought pita or potato chips, for serving

Note: Be sure to roast the garlic ahead of time. It takes 45 to 60 minutes in the oven, plus additional rest time. Roasting garlic brings out its natural sweetness. It is delicious in dips, salad dressings, other condiments, or just spread on some toasted crostini.

1. Place the cream cheese in a medium bowl. Using the back of a fork, mash the cheese until creamy. Add the roasted garlic, sour cream, and pepper and mash together until combined.

2. Transfer to a bowl, cover with plastic wrap, and refrigerate for 1 hour. Serve as desired with potato chips, veggies, or pita.

Homemade Potato Chips

Light, crisp, and oh so delicious, these homemade potato chips are a special treat. Double fried to a deep golden brown and finished with a sprinkling of kosher salt, they are perfect alongside Roasted Garlic Cream Cheese Dip (previous page)!

4 medium white potatoes
Vegetable oil, for frying
Kosher salt

Note: This is an extremely simple recipe, yet a little tedious. Make sure you have ample time to make these chips; they are worth the wait! Before cooking, the potatoes need to be cut and left to sit in cold water for 1 hour.

Variation:

Don't let your imagination stop you here. Make flavored chips by tossing them in your favorite seasoning—Taco Seasoning (page 177), perhaps?

1. Fill a large bowl filled halfway with cold water. Scrub the potatoes to make sure they are super-clean! Cut about ½ inch of the potato off one end. Using a mandoline on the thinnest setting, cut the potatoes, letting them fall into the cold water, making sure to use that hand guard!

2. Let the potatoes sit for 1 hour in the cold water.

3. Pour in enough oil to fill a large, deep, heavy-bottomed skillet to about a 2-inch depth and heat over medium heat, until it reaches 375°F. Place a wire cooling rack over a baking sheet.

4. Take about a dozen of the potato slices out of the water and pat them dry with paper towels, then carefully but quickly drop them into the hot oil. Using tongs, turn them over as soon as any browning occurs on the edges. Let cook until slightly browned all over. With tongs, remove them from the oil and let drain on the wire rack. Repeat until all the slices have been cooked; this is the end of the first fry.

5. The second fry goes by extremely fast. Take only about five chips at a time and drop them back in the oil. They are done when they are deep golden brown all over. Place them back on the wire rack and immediately sprinkle with kosher salt. Repeat until all the chips are double fried. Serve as desired.

Peel 'N' Eat Shrimp Cocktail

Living in Florida, I am very lucky to be able to purchase fresh-caught shrimp any day of the week. My favorite way to prepare it is a classic shrimp cocktail. However, boiling the shrimp plain just doesn't cut it for me, I like to bring the classic flavors of a seafood boil to my shrimp cocktail.

Serving the shrimp "peel-and-eat" flat-out saves you a whole lot of work! Let your friends and family do the hard part—the peeling. Served with homemade cocktail sauce, you can enjoy this fun appetizer hot or cold. Add drawn butter to the mix for an even more decadent treat.

24 ounces beer
4 cups water
4 whole garlic cloves, skins removed
½ large onion, cut in half, skin removed
1 cup baby carrots
2 celery stalks, cut in half
½ cup plus 2 teaspoons Old Bay seasoning
1 ½ pounds large, head-off shrimp
2 tablespoons unsalted butter, melted (optional)
Cocktail Sauce (page 176)
Lemon wedges, for serving (optional)

Note: If you plan on serving this dish chilled, I suggest making it at least 5 hours in advance so the shrimp can become really cold. This is my personal favorite way to eat them, but serving them warm makes them much easier to peel.

1. Place the beer, water, garlic, onion, carrots, celery, and ½ cup of the Old Bay seasoning in a large pot and bring to a boil. Allow to boil, covered, for 30 minutes.

2. Add the shrimp and cook until they are just done, 2 to 5 minutes. The flesh will be bright white, the shells will be pink, and the tails will curl. Drain and discard the cooking liquid.

3. Transfer the shrimp to a large bowl and add the remaining 2 teaspoons of Old Bay. If serving immediately, add the melted butter. Toss until coated. Serve immediately or lay out on a baking sheet and refrigerate for 5 hours, or until cold. Serve with cocktail sauce and lemon wedges, if desired. If serving cold, use the melted butter for dipping.

Variation:

Turn this into a true shrimp boil by adding whole baby red potatoes, smoked sausage, and corn on the cob.

Pro tip: The base of a cheese sauce is a good, old-fashioned béchamel. Butter, flour, and milk combine into a wonderful vehicle for your favorite melting cheeses. Try out different variations, such as adding fresh thyme instead of the dried seasonings listed here and using a smoked Gouda in place of the Cheddar. Pour over steamed vegetables of your choice. Talk about elevating boring veggies to the next level!

Ultimate Nachos

Nachos are a game day staple around our house. I make these at least once every two weeks during football season. They are so good. The real star of these nachos is the seasoned cheese sauce. Oh yes! It even goes great over Baked Potato Wedges (page 105) and Chili Cheese Dogs (page 61)!

For the nachos

½ pound lean ground beef (93/7)

1 tablespoon Taco Seasoning (page 177) or store-bought seasoning

½ cup canned black beans, drained and rinsed

¼ cup loosely packed fresh cilantro, roughly chopped, plus 1 tablespoon for garnish

½ cup water

5 ounces tortilla chips

½ cup shredded Mexican blend cheese

1 medium tomato, diced

1 tablespoon thinly sliced scallion

Sour cream, for serving

Green Salsa (page 170) or salsa of your choice, for serving

For the cheese sauce

2 tablespoons unsalted butter

2 tablespoons all-purpose flour

¼ teaspoon ground cumin

¼ teaspoon onion powder

¼ teaspoon garlic powder

¼ teaspoon paprika

1 cup whole milk

¾ cup shredded sharp Cheddar

1. Place the ground beef in a medium skillet over medium heat. Brown the beef, draining away any fat. Add the taco seasoning and black beans; stir to combine. Add the cilantro and water. Let simmer for 5 minutes, or until the sauce thickens and reduces by half.

2. While the meat is cooking, preheat the oven to 350°F and make the sauce: Melt the butter in a small saucepan over medium heat. Add the flour and spices. Whisk together until smooth and cook for 2 minutes, stirring constantly. Add the milk and whisk to combine. Bring to a boil and then cook until thick, 2 to 3 minutes. Remove from the heat, add the Cheddar, and stir to melt the cheese and combine the sauce. Set aside.

3. Layer one-third of the tortilla chips, one-third of the cooked meat, one-third of the cheese sauce, and one-third of the shredded cheese into a cast-iron skillet or oven-safe dish. Repeat in two more layers until everything is used up. Place in the oven to warm through and melt the shredded cheese, about 5 minutes. Top with the remaining 1 tablespoon cilantro, tomato, scallions, sour cream, and salsa as desired.

Romaine Wedge Salad

The ultimate salad, in my opinion, loaded with blue cheese, bacon, pickled onions, and homemade blue cheese dressing. All on top of a crispy head of romaine lettuce—dig in!

1 head romaine lettuce, cut in half lengthwise, core removed
3 slices bacon, cut into ½-inch dice, cooked crispy, then drained
1 small tomato, diced
Pickled Red Onions (page 171)
Blue Cheese Dressing (page 172)
Blue cheese crumbles

> Note: You will need to make the dressing and pickled onions ahead ahead of time. Both need some time in the fridge to rest.

1. Place one romaine half on each plate, then top with the bacon, tomato, onions, and as much dressing as you wish. Garnish with blue cheese crumbles.

Creamy Tomato Basil Soup with Parmesan Croutons

To me, there is nothing more comforting than a steaming bowl of soup on a chilly afternoon. It makes the perfect lunch or dinner with an epic Grilled Ham and Cheese Sandwich (page 75). One of my favorite soups of all time is a classic tomato basil. I kick this recipe up a notch by adding heavy cream for a luxurious consistency. The addition of Parmesan croutons (which are definitely necessary, in my opinion) just takes it to the next level!

For the soup

1 (28-ounce) can San Marzano
  plum tomatoes with basil
1 garlic clove, roughly chopped
1 cup chicken or vegetable stock
¼ cup prepared Basil Pesto (page 177)
½ teaspoon sugar
½ teaspoon kosher salt
3 cracks black pepper
1 tablespoon unsalted butter
1 tablespoon all-purpose flour
½ cup heavy cream

For the croutons

2 cups cubed French bread
  (1-inch cubes)
2 tablespoons Rosemary
  Garlic Olive Oil (page 175) or
  regular olive oil
4 tablespoons freshly grated
  Parmigiano-Reggiano
2 cracks black pepper

Variation: You can also make this soup in a small slow cooker. In step 1, add all of the ingredients to the slow cooker and cook on high for 2 to 3 hours or on low for at least 5 hours. Proceed with the recipe, as instructed, from step 2.

Make the soup:

1. Place the tomatoes, garlic, stock, 2 tablespoons of the pesto, and the sugar, salt, and pepper into a medium pot. Bring to a boil, cover, and simmer over medium-low heat for 2 hours. Blend with an immersion blender.

2. Melt the butter in a small sauté pan over medium heat, then add the flour. Whisk to combine into a paste. Add the cream, whisking to combine, and cook until thickened. Whisk into the soup to thicken. Drizzle with the remaining 2 tablespoons of pesto and serve with the croutons.

Make the croutons:

1. Preheat the oven to 375°F.

2. Toss together all the crouton ingredients in a large bowl and place on a baking sheet. Make sure none of the pieces of bread are touching. Bake for 10 minutes, or until golden brown. Make sure to check at around the 8-minute mark, as these croutons can turn extra golden brown superquick!

Pro tip: You will notice throughout this book that I use only San Marzano tomatoes if using canned. There is just something extra special about these tomatoes straight from Italy—I highly recommend them!

Fried Goat Cheese Salad

Goat cheese is one of my favorite cheeses. I love mixing it into sauces or crumbling it over warm grilled meat to give a great creamy tanginess to a dish. But one of my favorite ways to have it is fried. Coated in a panko bread-crumb crust, it is crunchy on the outside, warm and gooey in the center.

4 ounces goat cheese
¼ cup all-purpose flour
1 large egg, lightly beaten
½ cup panko bread crumbs
1 tablespoon freshly grated
   Parmesan
1 tablespoon vegetable oil
1 tablespoon unsalted butter
3 cups mixed greens
8 pickled beet slices
1 scallion, thinly sliced
¼ cup walnuts, roughly
   chopped
¼ cup thinly sliced cucumber
Lemon Vinaigrette (page 172)

1. Place the goat cheese in the freezer and chill for 15 minutes.

2. Set up a dredging station: Place the flour on a plate; the egg in a bowl; and mix the panko with the Parmesan on a separate plate.

3. Heat the oil and butter in a medium skillet over medium heat.

4. Cut the goat cheese into four equal disks. One at a time, coat the disks with the flour, then the egg, and then press them into the panko mixture.

5. Add the cheese to the pan and lightly fry until golden brown on all sides, 2 to 3 minutes per side. Drain on a paper towel and allow to cool slightly while you get the salad ready.

6. Toss the greens, beets, sliced scallion, walnuts, and cucumber in a large serving bowl (or make two individual salads), top with the fried goat cheese, and serve with the lemon vinaigrette.

Pro tip:
Chilling the goat cheese in the freezer makes slicing much easier!

The Main Course

Chicago-Style Deep Dish Pizza with Homemade Italian Sausage

Making this pizza instantly transports me back to Chicago. Don't let this recipe scare you—yes, there are quite a few steps, but it is worth it! (Thanks go to my dad for this recipe.)

For the dough

1 (¼-ounce) packet rapid-rise yeast
Pinch of sugar
¾ cup warm water
¼ cup vegetable oil
1 tablespoon extra virgin olive oil
4 tablespoons (½ stick) unsalted butter, melted and cooled
¾ teaspoon kosher salt
¼ cup cornmeal
1½ cups plus 6 tablespoons all-purpose flour

Note: For this recipe I recommend using a stand mixer to make the dough. If all you have is a hand mixer, you can still make this recipe. Follow the directions as is, but use a large bowl. Warning: Your arms will most likely get tired!

Make the dough:

1. Place the yeast, sugar, warm water, vegetable and olive oils, and butter in the bowl of a stand mixer fitted with the hook attachment (see note). Stir to combine, then let sit until bubbles start to form, about 5 minutes. Mix together the salt, cornmeal, and flour in a separate bowl. With the mixer on low speed, gradually add the flour mixture to the yeast mixture, scraping down the sides of the bowl as necessary.

2. When all of the flour mixture is incorporated, switch to high speed and beat for 6 minutes. Turn off the mixer. Cover the bowl with a clean towel and place in a warm spot, such as a microwave or an oven with the light turned on. Let rise for 1 hour, or until the dough has doubled in size. While the dough is rising, make the other pizza components.

continued

Pro tip: You are making homemade sausage in this recipe. Note that you are not cooking the sausage beforehand. Don't get scared; it *will* cook fully in the oven.

For the sausage

½ pound ground pork
¼ teaspoon dried oregano
¼ teaspoon dried basil
2 garlic cloves, minced
1 ½ teaspoons fennel seeds
   (crushed in a mortar and
   pestle or coffee grinder)
¼ teaspoon kosher salt
2 cracks black pepper

For the sauce

1 ¾ cups (half of a 28-ounce
   can) canned San Marzano
   plum tomatoes, crushed by
   hand, cores removed
1 ½ teaspoons dried basil
1 ½ teaspoons dried oregano
½ teaspoon garlic powder
1 tablespoon freshly grated
   Parmigiano-Reggiano

For the assembly

4 tablespoons (½ stick)
   unsalted butter
Cooking spray
1 pound mozzarella, sliced
2 tablespoons extra virgin olive oil
¼ cup freshly grated Parmigiano-
   Reggiano

Make the sausage:

1. Combine all the sausage ingredients in a bowl and mix well by hand. Store in the refrigerator until ready to assemble the pizza.

Make the sauce:

1. Combine all the sauce ingredients in a bowl and mix well by hand. Store in the refrigerator until ready to assemble the pizza.

Assemble and bake the pizza:

1. Preheat the oven to 400°F. Grease two 9-inch round cake pans with the butter.

2. Place half of the dough in each pan. Spray your hands with cooking spray and work the dough into the bottom of the pan and slightly up the sides.

3. Layer half of the cheese evenly in each pan, pressing the cheese lightly into the lower crease of the dough where it extends up the side of the pan. Layer half of the sausage evenly in each pan, making little dollops of it all over the cheese. Top evenly with the sauce. Drizzle 1 tablespoon of the olive oil over each pizza, and finish off with the Parmigiano-Reggiano.

4. Bake for 40 to 45 minutes, until the crust is golden brown and everything is bubbly. Remove from the oven and place the pans on a wire rack. Let the pizzas cool for 10 to 15 minutes before slicing, to let them set up. Slice in the pan and serve.

Spaghetti and Meatballs with Sausage

MAKES 6 TO
8 SERVINGS
(THIS IS ONE OF
THOSE RECIPES
WHERE *IF* THERE
ARE ANY LEFTOVERS,
IT IS BETTER THE
NEXT DAY)

All the women on my mother's side have this dish down. I have fond memories of having mostaccioli noodles with my grandma's homemade sauce every time I would go over and visit. As we all do with recipes, this has been tweaked here and there as it has been passed down. Here is my version . . . and shhh, I think it might be the best! (Sorry, Mom, Auntie, and Grandma!)

For the sauce

2 links Italian sausage
1 tablespoon extra virgin olive oil
1 (6-ounce) can tomato paste
1 tablespoon dried oregano
1 teaspoon onion powder
2 (28-ounce) cans crushed San Marzano tomatoes with basil
1 head Roasted Garlic (page 174)
0.5 ounce fresh basil, leaves torn (1 cup loosely packed leaves)
1 cup freshly grated Parmigiano-Reggiano
½ teaspoon sugar
2 tablespoons dry red wine

For the meatballs

1 pound lean ground beef (93/7)
1 teaspoon onion powder
1 teaspoon garlic powder
½ cup freshly grated Parmigiano-Reggiano
1 large egg, lightly beaten
¼ cup panko bread crumbs
5 cracks black pepper

Cooked pasta of your choice, for serving

Make the sauce:

1. Heat the olive oil in a large saucepan over medium heat. Add the sausage and fry until browned on all sides. Remove from the pot and set aside.

2. Add the tomato paste, oregano, and onion powder to the pot. Let fry in the oil until fragrant, stirring constantly, 2 minutes. Add the rest of the sauce ingredients, except the wine, to the pot. Mix well until combined, then add the sausage back to the pot. Cover, lower heat to low, and simmer, stirring occasionally, for at least 4 hours.

Make the meatballs:

1. Preheat the oven to 425°F.

2. While the sauce is simmering, place the meatball ingredients in a medium bowl and mix by hand. Roll about 2 tablespoons at a time into balls, placing them on a baking sheet. Bake for 20 minutes, or until the meatballs are a golden brown.

continued

3. Place the meatballs in the sauce. Return the baking sheet to the oven and turn on the broiler. Broil for 3 minutes under the highest setting. This will make all the leftover bits from the meatballs get nice and golden brown. Remove the pan from the oven; be careful as the oils are extremely hot.

4. Deglaze the pan with the red wine, scraping all the little bits off the bottom of the pan, and pour everything into the pot of sauce.

5. Stir to combine and let everything continue to simmer for the full 4 hours, or longer if you have the time. Serve over pasta of your choice.

Variation:

Sometimes I don't have the time to stir the sauce as often as needed. If this is the case for you, make the sauce in a large, lidded, oven-safe pot. After everything is added, including the meatballs, place the whole pot, covered, in the oven at 250°F. Let it slow cook in there for you!

Pro tip:

You might find a few techniques in this recipe odd. Trust me on this; follow the directions and experience the most flavorful sauce ever!

Creamy Shrimp and Grits

Grits are a staple breakfast food in the South. But shrimp and grits can be enjoyed at any time of the day! Creamy grits are topped with large shrimp that have been sautéed in butter, herbs, and a dash of cream.

For the grits

2 cups water
½ teaspoon kosher salt
2 tablespoons unsalted butter
½ cup old-fashioned grits
½ cup heavy cream
½ teaspoon finely chopped
    fresh parsley
½ teaspoon fresh thyme leaves
1 tablespoon thinly sliced
    chives
2 cracks black pepper

For the shrimp

1 tablespoon unsalted butter
½ teaspoon extra virgin olive oil
½ pound large shrimp, cleaned
    and shells removed
1 garlic clove, minced
¼ teaspoon kosher salt
2 cracks black pepper
2 tablespoons heavy cream
½ teaspoon finely chopped
    fresh parsley
1 teaspoon thinly sliced chives
Lemon zest, for garnish
    (optional)

Make the grits:

1. Combine the water, salt, and butter in a medium saucepan over high heat and bring to a boil. Slowly add the grits, stirring as you go. Lower the heat to low, cover, and cook, stirring occasionally, for 15 minutes.

2. Add the cream and cook, stirring occasionally, until most of the liquid is absorbed and the grits have thickened, about another 5 minutes. Remove from the heat and stir in the herbs and pepper. The mixture will thicken more as it cools.

Make the shrimp:

1. Heat the butter and olive oil in a medium skillet over high heat. Add the shrimp and garlic and cook just until the shrimp are cooked through, 3 to 4 minutes. Add the garlic, salt, pepper, cream, and herbs and stir to combine.

2. Serve the shrimp on top of the grits, garnished with the lemon zest.

Pro tip:

Leaving the tail on the shrimp makes for a pretty presentation. But, to make this dish easier to eat, I suggest removing the entire shell before cooking.

Slow Cooker Pulled Pork Sliders

MAKES
3 TO 4
SERVINGS

Making pulled pork at home is easier than you might think! Slow cooked, sprinkled with delicious seasonings, mixed with whatever BBQ sauce you wish, and served on mini slider buns with Pickled Red Onions (page 171)— time for a mini cookout!

1 ½ teaspoons packed light
   brown sugar
½ teaspoon salt
½ teaspoon ground cumin
¼ teaspoon garlic powder
¼ teaspoon onion powder
¼ teaspoon paprika
3 cracks black pepper
1 pound pork loin, excess fat
   removed
Your favorite BBQ sauce
Pickled Red Onions (page 171)
   or other toppings of choice

1. Mix together the brown sugar, salt, spices, and pepper in a small bowl. Rub this all over the pork loin. Place the seasoned pork directly in a slow cooker. Cook on low for 8 to 10 hours, until fork-tender.

2. Pull the pork and mix with your desired amount of BBQ sauce. Place the meat in the slider buns and garnish with pickled red onions or other toppings, as desired.

Grilled Chicken Tacos

We have tacos at least once a week at our house. I think that is the same for a lot of families. I mean, hello, tacos are flat-out amazing. But the traditional homemade ground beef version can get a little repetitious sometimes. So, when taco Tuesday rolls around and you're not feeling the same old, same old, whip out this recipe. These have been called, and I quote, "the best tacos I have ever tasted." And, no, it was not me saying that! The first time I made these tacos, Jeremy fell head over heels in love with them. And I haven't looked back since. My motto is, when you create a winner, you don't go messing around with it and changing the recipe.

2 tablespoons packed light
   brown sugar
1 tablespoon white vinegar
1 tablespoon water
1 tablespoon roughly chopped
   fresh cilantro
2 teaspoons ground cumin
1 teaspoon paprika
1 teaspoon garlic powder
1 teaspoon onion powder
5 cracks black pepper
½ teaspoon kosher salt
1 boneless, skinless chicken
   breast or 2 boneless, skinless
   chicken thighs
4 small flour tortillas
Your favorite toppings;
   I suggest Green Salsa (page
   170), sour cream, diced
   tomato, and fresh cilantro

Note: The chicken needs to
marinate for at least 3 hours,
up to overnight.

1. Place the brown sugar, vinegar, water, cilantro, cumin, paprika, garlic powder, onion powder, black pepper, and salt in a small bowl and whisk together to combine. Place the chicken in a medium bowl and pour the marinade on top, making sure to coat the chicken. Cover with plastic wrap and refrigerate for at least 3 hours, up to overnight.

2. Prepare a grill (or a grill pan). Place the chicken on the grill and brush with the marinade (discard any remaining marinade). Grill the chicken over medium-low heat for 15 to 20 minutes for breast meat or 10 minutes for thighs, or until its internal temperature reaches 165°F.

3. Let the chicken rest for 5 to 10 minutes after taking it off the grill. During this time, place the tortillas directly on the grates to warm through.

4. Slice the chicken against the grain and place it in the tortillas with your toppings of choice.

Pro tip: Letting the steak sit out for 30 minutes prior to cooking allows it to come to room temperature. This makes sure it will cook through evenly.

Marinated Grilled Rib-Eye Steaks

A simple and easy marinade takes an already amazing cut of meat to the next level. These steaks are perfect for special-occasion meals or when you just want a treat! This is my go-to steak marinade. I may be known to whip it out when I want to be extra sweet on Jeremy. To make it a true steak house experience: serve with a Romaine Wedge Salad (page 29), Rustic Roasted Garlic Mashed Potatoes (page 101), and Grilled Asparagus (page 113).

1 pound bone-in rib-eye steak, boneless or other cuts (get as close to 1 pound as you can)
8 cracks black pepper
2 teaspoons light brown sugar
½ teaspoon Montreal steak seasoning
½ teaspoon kosher salt
1 tablespoon Worcestershire sauce
1 tablespoon unsalted butter
Chopped fresh parsley, for garnish (optional)

Note: Steaks need to marinate for at least 3 hours; leave enough time in advance for this recipe. And don't let the name of this recipe deter you—this marinade is amazing on any cut of steak!

1. Place the steak on a large plate and sprinkle with the pepper, brown sugar, Montreal seasoning, and salt. Using your hands, rub the flavorings all over the steak. Drizzle one side with half of the Worcestershire sauce, flip over, and drizzle on the rest, making sure the steak is coated. Wrap with plastic wrap and refrigerate for at least 3 hours, up to overnight, to marinate.

2. Before cooking, set the steak out on the countertop to bring to room temperature, about 30 minutes. This will ensure an even cook.

3. Prepare a grill; I suggest charcoal for this recipe (alternatively, you can cook the steak in a grill pan on the stovetop).

4. Sear the steak on both sides until cooked to your liking: about 5 minutes on each side for medium, or until the internal temperature reaches 145°F.

5. Remove from the heat and add the butter; let it melt over the steak while it rests for 5 minutes. Add the parsley, if using, and serve.

Short Rib Shepherd's Pie

I love making classic recipes my own. Traditionally, shepherd's pie is made with lamb. Here, I have substituted beef short ribs, combining two dishes that are the epitome of comfort food into one tasty dish!

1 ½ pounds beef short ribs
   (or close to that weight)
Kosher salt
Cracked black pepper
3 tablespoons all-purpose flour
1 tablespoon vegetable oil
2 tablespoons red wine
   (optional)
1 ½ cups beef stock
2 garlic cloves, skin removed
   and smashed with the flat
   part of a knife
4 sprigs fresh thyme
1 sprig fresh rosemary
1 bay leaf
1 tablespoon unsalted butter
½ cup diced white onion
½ cup diced carrot
½ cup diced celery
1 recipe Rustic Roasted Garlic
   Mashed Potatoes (page 101)
   or 1 ½ cups other mashed
   potatoes
½ cup frozen peas

Note: Mashed potatoes (see page 101 for my rustic roasted garlic recipe) are needed as a topping on this dish. Make sure you have enough on hand, or make them as the short ribs cook.

1. Season the short ribs generously on all sides with the salt and pepper. Dredge the ribs in 2 tablespoons of the flour, tapping off the excess. Set aside.

2. Heat an 8-inch cast-iron skillet over medium heat. Add and heat the vegetable oil. In batches, sear the short ribs until golden brown on all sides, transferring the ribs to a plate as they cook.

3. Meanwhile, preheat the oven to 325°F.

4. Remove the skillet from the heat and place the ribs back in the skillet. Add the wine, stock, garlic, and herbs. Cover tightly with foil and roast in the oven for 2 to 2 ½ hours, until the meat can be shredded off the bone.

5. While the short ribs are cooking, prepare the mashed potatoes if you do not already have them on hand.

6. When the meat is done cooking, remove it from the pan and place it on a plate; set aside. Using a strainer, strain the liquid from the pan into a bowl and discard any solids. Skim the fat off the top of the liquid and discard; set the cooking liquid aside.

7. Melt the butter in the cast-iron skillet over medium heat. Add the onion, carrot, and celery. Cook, stirring occasionally, until the onion is translucent, 8 to 10 minutes. While the vegetables are cooking, shred the short rib meat and discard the bones.

Pro tip:
Searing off the short ribs before cooking in the oven gives an extra richness to this dish. Do not skip this step! I know you will be tempted, but trust me on this.

8. Add the remaining tablespoon of flour to the vegetable mixture and stir to combine. Add the cooking liquid and cook until thickened, 3 to 5 minutes. Add the shredded meat and the peas. Top with the mashed potatoes. Broil on high in the oven for 8 minutes, or until golden brown on top.

Pro tip: This recipe is all about the sauce. It sounds odd, but we are basically making a soy sauce–flavored caramel. I've told you this before . . . trust me.

Sweet Soy-Glazed Chicken

My go-to take-out-in recipe! I get asked to make this every time I have family visiting or if I'm visiting them. I've been told it's better than any restaurant version they've ever had . . . try it out and be the judge yourself! For the full effect, serve with Fried Rice (page 92).

For the chicken

4 boneless, skinless chicken thighs or 2 boneless, skinless chicken breasts, cut into 1-inch pieces
¼ teaspoon onion powder
¼ teaspoon garlic powder
2 tablespoons cornstarch
Vegetable oil, for frying
Fried Rice (page 92), for serving (optional)

For the sauce

2 teaspoons vegetable oil
1 garlic clove, minced
¼ cup soy sauce
1 cup light brown sugar
1 teaspoon white vinegar
3 cracks black pepper

Note: Feel free to use dark or white meat chicken for this recipe or a combination of the two.

Dredge the chicken:

1. Place the chicken in a gallon zip-top plastic bag, add the onion and garlic powder, and toss to coat. Add the cornstarch, seal the bag, and shake to coat the chicken. Set aside.

2. Pour enough oil into a large, deep skillet to come about ½ inch up the side of the pan. Heat over medium heat.

Make the sauce:

1. While the oil is heating, heat 2 tablespoons of vegetable oil in a small saucepan over medium heat. Add the garlic and cook until fragrant, about 1 minute. Add the remaining sauce ingredients and whisk to combine. Let the sauce cook at a slight simmer, stirring occasionally, while you cook the chicken. Be careful; if it gets too hot, it will boil over the sides of the pot.

2. When the oil in the skillet is hot, place the chicken pieces in the oil in a single layer, making sure they are not touching. You will need to cook the chicken in batches. Cook on one side for about 3 minutes, then flip with tongs. The chicken is done when its internal temperature reaches 165°F. Transfer the cooked chicken to a paper towel–lined plate. Repeat until all the chicken is done.

3. The sauce is done when it is thickened and there is the *slightest* burnt sugar smell to it, like caramel. Toss the chicken in the sauce and serve with fried rice, if desired.

Taco Patty Melts

I have always loved the idea of fusion recipes. Mixing together two elements of different dishes and coming out with something totally unexpected just really appeals to me. Sometimes I crave a good patty melt and I thought it would be fun to upgrade it to the next level. Adding a taco twist really elevates this sandwich into something phenomenal! Melty cheese, peppers, and onions mixed with ground beef seasoned with homemade taco seasoning—a little bite of heaven, if you ask me!

1 tablespoon unsalted butter, divided

½ cup julienned yellow bell pepper

¼ cup julienned white onion

½ pound lean ground beef (93/7)

1 tablespoon Taco Seasoning (page 177)

½ cup water

1 tablespoon roughly chopped fresh cilantro

4 slices crusty bread (sourdough would be amazing here)

1 cup shredded Mexican blend cheese

Note: Making the taco seasoning ahead of time will save you time while cooking this recipe. Keep the remaining seasoning in an airtight container for use next time! Serve with your favorite dipping sauces, such as sour cream or Green Salsa (page 170).

1. Heat a medium skillet over medium heat until hot. Add half of the butter, let it melt, and add the pepper and onion. Cook until softened, 3 minutes. Add the ground beef and cook through, about 5 minutes.

2. Add the taco seasoning and stir to combine. Add the water and cilantro, stir to combine, and simmer for 5 to 7 minutes, or until a thick sauce forms and reduces by half.

3. Use the remaining 1½ teaspoons of butter to butter one side of each slice of bread. Heat a separate skillet over medium heat. Place the bread, butter side down, in the pan. Layer with a quarter of the cheese, half of the meat mixture, another quarter of the cheese, and another slice of bread, buttered-side up. Cover and let brown on the bottom side, about 3 minutes. Flip over, cover, and let the other side of the sandwich brown. Repeat to make the second sandwich.

Slow Cooker Chunky Beef Stew

Another comforting classic! Made in a slow cooker so it couldn't be easier, this beef stew can be put together the night before, placed in the slow cooker in the morning, cooked while you are away, and BAM! dinner is served. Classic Yeast Rolls (page 123) make the perfect accompaniment.

1 pound stew beef
½ teaspoon kosher salt
5 cracks black pepper
2 tablespoons all-purpose flour
1 tablespoon vegetable oil
1 cup diced red potatoes
   (about 4 small potatoes)
1 cup chopped carrot
½ cup thinly sliced celery
½ cup diced white onion
2 garlic cloves, minced
1 sprig fresh rosemary
2 sprigs fresh thyme
2 bay leaves
2½ cups beef stock
½ cup dry red wine
2 tablespoons tomato paste
½ cup frozen peas

1. Season the beef with salt and pepper; coat with the flour. Heat the oil in a large skillet over medium-high heat and brown the meat. Make sure it is golden brown on all sides. Place the meat in a slow cooker.

2. Add the remaining ingredients, except the peas, to the slow cooker. Stir to combine everything. Cook on high for 5 hours. Take off the lid and cook on high for an additional hour, removing the bay leaves and herb stems.

3. During the last 10 minutes of cooking, add the frozen peas to warm through. Taste, and adjust the seasoning if necessary.

Brown Sugar Meat Loaf

We are huge fans of meat loaf in our family. I know that sometimes it gets a bad rap. Try out this recipe—there is a touch of sweetness from the addition of brown sugar that really sets this dish off! Serve with Rosemary Roasted Fingerling Potatoes (page 91) and Broccoli Rice Casserole (page 99).

1 large egg, lightly beaten
1 teaspoon onion powder
1 teaspoon garlic powder
1 tablespoon Worcestershire sauce
¼ cup panko bread crumbs
¼ teaspoon kosher salt
5 cracks black pepper
2 tablespoons packed light brown sugar, divided
¼ cup ketchup, divided
1 pound lean ground beef (93/7)

1. Preheat the oven to 425°F.

2. Place all the ingredients, except the sugar, ketchup, and beef, in a medium bowl and mix to combine. Add half of the brown sugar and half of the ketchup. Mix everything together. Add the beef and, with your hands, mix everything until combined. Do not overmix.

3. Form the meat into a loaf on a baking sheet. Mix together the remaining brown sugar and ketchup in a small bowl and brush all over the meat loaf. Bake for 35 to 40 minutes, until the internal temperature reaches 165°F.

Chili Cheese Dogs

A cookout favorite! This is a beanless chili, similar to a Cincinnati chili, which ends up being more of a sauce than a chunky chili. It goes perfectly on hot dogs. When you top it with finely shredded Cheddar and onions, you have a summer staple.

For the chili
½ pound lean ground beef (97/3)
½ teaspoon chili powder
¼ teaspoon ground cumin
Pinch of garlic powder
Pinch of onion powder
Pinch of ground ginger
Pinch of ground cinnamon
2 cracks black pepper
Pinch of kosher salt
Splash of soy sauce
Splash of Worcestershire sauce
½ cup tomato sauce
3 tablespoons ketchup
2 tablespoons water
½ teaspoon prepared yellow mustard

For the assembly
4 to 6 hot dogs
4 to 6 hot-dog buns
1 cup finely shredded sharp Cheddar
Prepared mustard (optional)
Diced white onion (optional)

> Note: Yes, it looks like there are some crazy spices in this recipe. Plus, not a lot of each one is added; trust me, you need to add everything for this flavor profile!

1. Make the chili first: Brown the ground beef in a medium saucepan over medium heat. Use a potato masher to break up the beef; you want it as finely ground as possible. Add all the dried spices, and the pepper and salt. Cook for 30 seconds, or until fragrant.

2. Add the three sauces, ketchup, water, and mustard, stir to combine, cover, and cook over medium-low heat, stirring occasionally, for 30 minutes.

3. While the chili is cooking, grill the hot dogs. Place the hot dogs in the buns, top with the chili, and add Cheddar, mustard, and diced onion, as desired.

Cranberry Walnut Rotisserie Chicken Salad

Chicken salad is a go-to lunch option in our house. I love using leftover store-bought rotisserie chicken to make ours. Add dried cranberries and walnuts and toss it all in Garlic Salad Dressing (page 173) and you have one flavorful chicken salad!

2 cups diced rotisserie chicken
½ cup diced celery
1 scallion, thinly sliced
1 tablespoon finely chopped
   fresh parsley
2 tablespoons dried
   cranberries
2 tablespoons chopped
   walnuts
¼ cup Garlic Salad Dressing
   (page 173)
2 large croissants, sliced
   lengthwise

Note: This recipe calls for my multipurpose Garlic Salad Dressing (page 173); make sure you have this on hand before you start.

1. Mix together all the ingredients, except the croissants.

2. Pile the chicken salad on the croissants and serve.

Variations:
This is another great base recipe; feel free to experiment with additions here. Blue cheese crumbles, Pickled Red Onions (page 171), and arugula would be extra yummy!

Caprese Pizza

MAKES 2
(8- TO 9-INCH)
PIZZAS

Homemade pizza crust topped with Basil Pesto (page 177), Roma tomatoes, and fresh mozzarella—simple and classic.

For the dough
1 ⅛ teaspoons (½ packet) rapid-rise yeast
¾ cup warm water
2 tablespoons unsalted butter, melted and cooled to room temperature
1 tablespoon extra virgin olive oil
½ tablespoon sugar
4 cups all-purpose flour, plus more for dusting
½ teaspoon kosher salt

For the pizza
1 to 2 tablespoons cornmeal
4 tablespoons Basil Pesto (page 177)
2 Roma tomatoes, thinly sliced
8 ounces fresh mozzarella, grated by hand

Notes: This recipe calls for a stand mixer. This will make the job of making the dough much easier and faster. However, a hand mixer can be used in its place; following the directions the same way.

Waiting for the dough to rise multiple times can be tedious. Be patient; it's worth it!

Make the dough:

1. Place the yeast, water, butter, olive oil, and sugar in the bowl of a stand mixer fitted with the hook attachment. Mix slightly to combine, then let sit for about 5 minutes, until bubbles start to form.

2. Add 1 cup of the flour and the salt. Mix on medium speed, scraping the sides as needed. Keep adding additional flour a little at a time until the dough starts to rub the sides of the mixer dry. You want to make sure the majority of the dough is attached around the hook and not sticking to the sides.

3. Place the dough in the bottom of the bowl and cover the bowl with plastic wrap. Set in a dry, warm place, such as a microwave or oven with the light on, to rise for 30 to 45 minutes, until the dough has doubled in size.

4. On a floured work surface, turn out the dough and push down to release the bubbles slightly. Cut the dough in half and form into balls. Cover with a clean kitchen towel and allow to rest for 30 minutes on the work surface.

Make the pizza:

1. Roll out one dough ball on the floured surface, using a rolling pin, until it forms an 8- to 9-inch circle. Lightly coat a pizza peel with the cornmeal and place the dough directly on top. Cover with a clean kitchen towel and let rest for 20 minutes. (Yes, this means the other half of the dough will be sitting for additional time; don't worry, it's fine!)

continued

2. Meanwhile, preheat the oven with a pizza stone to 425°F. Place 2 tablespoons of the pesto on the dough and coat it evenly. Add half of the sliced tomatoes and half of the cheese. Place on the pizza stone and bake for 12 to 15 minutes, until the crust is golden brown and the cheese starts to brown.

3. Repeat the process with the other ball of dough. Wait about 10 minutes before cutting into the pizzas, to let them set.

Pro tip:
I highly suggest using a pizza stone here. It helps achieve a nice, crispy crust. A pizza peel will make your job a whole lot easier as well. If you do not have these items, a regular baking sheet will work for the cooking of the pizza, and a cutting board or flat baking sheet will work in place of the peel.

Creamy Chicken Potpies

This meal is just like a warm hug. It is so comforting and especially satisfying on a cold night, all bundled up. I have to say, the star of this dish is the crust. Made with cream cheese, it is so flavorful that you need a bit in every bite!

For the filling

1 split chicken breast
1 cup chicken stock
2 bay leaves
4 tablespoons (½ stick)
   unsalted butter
¼ cup diced white onion
¼ cup diced carrot
¼ cup diced celery
1 garlic clove, minced
½ teaspoon fresh thyme leaves
¼ cup all-purpose flour
½ cup milk
½ teaspoon kosher salt
8 cracks black pepper
½ cup frozen peas

Make the filling:

1. Place the chicken, stock, and bay leaves in a medium pot. Bring to a boil, cover, and let simmer over medium-low heat for 1 hour. Remove the chicken from the pot and let cool until you can touch it. Meanwhile, strain the liquid from the pot and set aside. Remove the skin and bones from the chicken and dice into 1-inch pieces; set aside.

2. Preheat the oven to 375°F.

3. Melt the butter in a large, deep skillet over medium-low heat. Add the onion, carrot, celery, garlic, and thyme. Stir to coat with the butter, cover, and cook, stirring occasionally, for 10 minutes.

4. Add the flour to the pan and stir to combine. Increase the heat to medium and slowly add the milk, ½ cup of the reserved chicken cooking liquid, and the salt and pepper. Stir and let bubble until thickened. Add the diced chicken back to the pan along with the peas and coat everything with the sauce. Divide the mixture equally between two 4-inch-wide by 2-inch-deep oven-safe dishes. Set aside.

continued

For the crust

1 cup all-purpose flour, plus more for dusting

½ teaspoon kosher salt

8 tablespoons (1 stick) unsalted butter, cut into ½-inch cubes

4 ounces cream cheese, cut into ½-inch cubes

Make the crust:

1. Place all the crust ingredients in a medium bowl. Roll the flour, butter, and cream cheese between your fingers until the mixture is crumbly but combined. Turn out onto a floured work surface and press into a ball. Divide into two equal pieces. Roll out each piece with a rolling pin, flouring the top of the dough and the rolling pin, until a little more than 4 inches in diameter and ¼ inch thick. Drape each piece over a filled baking dish. Using a knife, make a tiny hole in the top of each crust for steam to escape.

2. Bake for 30 to 35 minutes, until the crust is golden brown.

Variation:

Feel free to add any additional veggies you would like. You can also use two chicken thighs instead of the breast. Make just one pie by placing the filling in an 8-inch baking dish and covering the whole thing with one large crust. The baking time might exceed 35 minutes for a golden-brown crust on a larger pie.

Cheesy Bacon and Kale Quiche

Using the same cream cheese crust from our Creamy Chicken Potpies (page 67), this quiche is definitely a flavorful beauty. Loaded with cheese, bacon, and eggs, it is a great breakfast option. Also a show-stopping brunch, lunch, or dinner with small side salad!

2 slices thick-cut bacon, cut into ½-inch dice
¼ cup diced white onion
½ cup diced potato (use any type of potato you wish)
2 tablespoons water
1 garlic clove, minced
½ teaspoon fresh thyme leaves
1 cup packed, chopped kale leaves
1 recipe Creamy Chicken Potpie crust (page 67)
2 large eggs, lightly beaten
⅓ cup milk
¾ cup shredded sharp Cheddar
Pinch of kosher salt
5 cracks black pepper

1. Preheat the oven to 350°F.

2. Render the bacon and cook until crispy in a medium skillet over medium-low heat. Let the bacon drain on a paper towel, reserving 2 teaspoons of the bacon fat in the pan. Cook the onion in the fat for 2 minutes, until slightly translucent. Add the potato, water, garlic, and thyme, cover, and cook, stirring occasionally, for 10 minutes.

3. Add the kale, cover, and let it wilt, about 2 minutes. Remove from the heat and set aside.

4. Roll out the crust to fit into an 8-inch cast-iron pan or oven-safe dish. Set aside.

5. Combine the eggs, milk, half of the cheese, and the salt and pepper in a large bowl. Add the vegetable mixture and stir everything together. Pour into the crust and top with the remaining cheese. Bake for 30 to 35 minutes, until the eggs are set and the crust is golden brown.

Variation:

This is another base recipe in which you can add or omit ingredients, such as leftover rotisserie chicken or roasted red peppers, as you wish. Have fun!

Fish 'N' Chips

Fish fillets dipped in a simple batter and fried to golden brown deliciousness. Served with classic Tartar Sauce (page 176), lemon wedges, and Baked Potato Wedges (page 105). One of my favorite guilty pleasures!

Vegetable oil, for frying
1 pound cod fillets, cut into
    1-inch strips
¼ teaspoon garlic powder
½ teaspoon paprika
½ teaspoon seasoned salt
½ teaspoon baking powder
¼ teaspoon baking soda
⅔ cup plus 1 tablespoon all-
    purpose flour
¾ cup cold water
Tartar Sauce (page 176)
Lemon wedges, for serving
    (optional)

> Note: I highly recommend using cod fillets for this recipe. If they are hard to find, you can substitute another firm white fish, such as haddock. You can also use defrosted frozen cod fillets, but for the best results I prefer to use fresh fish whenever possible.

1. Pour in enough oil to fill a large, deep skillet to about a 1-inch depth and heat over medium heat.

2. While the oil is heating, place the fish in a large bowl. Add the dried seasonings and toss the fish to make sure it is coated. Add the baking powder, baking soda, and flour and mix together with the fish so it is coated. Add the water, a little at a time, stirring everything by hand. You may not need to use all of the water; you want the batter to be the same consistency as pancake batter. Do not overmix.

3. Letting any excess batter drip off first, carefully add the cod pieces to the oil one at a time, so they are not touching. Cook until golden brown, flipping occasionally. Remove from the oil and transfer to a paper towel–lined plate, blotting off any excess oil. Then, transfer the fish to a wire rack that has been placed on a baking sheet. Continue with all the pieces of fish.

4. Serve with tartar sauce and lemon wedges, if desired.

Pro tip:
Make the tartar sauce at least an hour ahead of time and let it chill in the refrigerator. This will help to make all the flavors blend together.

Grilled Ham and Cheese Sandwiches

Who doesn't love a grilled cheese sandwich? They instantly take me back to my childhood! Here I have elevated them to a more grown-up version. Tavern ham, Pepper Jack, and white Cheddar take the classic sandwich to the next level. I suggest serving these with Creamy Tomato Basil Soup (page 30), Baked Potato Wedges (page 105), or Creamy Tangy Potato Salad (page 107).

4 slices crusty bread of your choice
2 tablespoons unsalted butter, at room temperature
4 slices white Cheddar
½ pound sliced deli tavern ham
4 slices Pepper Jack

1. Place a griddle pan over medium-low heat. Butter one side of a slice of bread with ½ tablespoon of the butter and place directly on the griddle, butter side down. Layer with two slices of the Cheddar cheese, half of the ham, 2 slices of Pepper Jack, and another slice of bread. Butter the top slice of bread with ½ tablespoon of butter.

2. Cook for 5 to 8 minutes per side, turning once, until golden brown and melty.

3. Repeat to make the second sandwich.

Panko Fried Shrimp

A light, crispy, crunchy exterior makes this shrimp recipe stand out from the rest. Serve with a simple Cocktail Sauce (page 176), lemon wedges, and Creamy Tangy Potato Salad (page 107) and your summer night-in is complete!

Vegetable oil, for frying
¼ cup all-purpose flour
½ teaspoon onion powder
½ teaspoon garlic powder
½ teaspoon paprika
1 teaspoon salt
1 large egg, lightly beaten with a splash of water
½ cup panko bread crumbs
1 pound large shrimp, peeled and deveined
Cocktail Sauce (page 176), for serving
Lemon wedges, for serving

1. Pour in enough oil to fill a large, deep skillet to about a ½-inch depth and heat over medium heat.

2. Set up your breading station: Place the flour in a plate and season with half of the onion powder, garlic powder, paprika, and salt; stir to combine. Next, place the egg mixture in a bowl. Last, fill a second plate with the bread crumbs and remaining onion powder, garlic powder, paprika, and salt; mix to combine.

3. When the oil is hot, start breading the shrimp by placing them, one by one, into the flour mixture to coat. Dip into the egg, then press into the bread crumbs. Shake off any excess crumbs and place the shrimp in the hot oil. Cook until golden brown, 2 to 3 minutes per side, then drain on a paper towel–lined plate. Serve with cocktail sauce and lemon wedges.

Pro tip:
This recipe includes that messy frying process you always hear about. To keep down the mess, wear gloves!

Slow Cooker French Dip Sandwiches

Yum! *One of my favorite sandwiches of* all time*! Super tender beef,
amazingly flavorful broth, melty provolone, caramelized onion . . . all
on garlic bread! Yes, I can eat this every day.*

1 pound London broil, cut into
    large chunks
1 teaspoon dried oregano
¾ teaspoon onion powder
¾ teaspoon garlic powder
¾ teaspoon Montreal steak
    seasoning
2 garlic cloves, smashed
2 bay leaves
2 cups beef stock
1 tablespoon unsalted butter
1 small white onion, thinly
    sliced
Pinch of kosher salt
1 large loaf garlic bread (can
    be frozen or from the bakery
    section at the grocery store)
4 slices provolone

1. Place the meat in a slow cooker, sprinkle with the dried seasonings, and add the garlic, bay leaves, and stock to the pot. Cover and cook on low for 8 hours. Remove the meat and discard the bay leaves. Shred the meat and reserve the cooking liquid as a dip for your sandwiches.

2. Thirty minutes before ready to serve, preheat the oven to 400°F.

3. Melt the butter in a small skillet, add the onion and coat with the butter, and season with the salt. Cook over medium-low heat, stirring occasionally, for 30 minutes. The onion should be soft with a light golden color. While the onion is cooking, prepare the garlic bread as needed.

4. Top the bread with the meat, add the caramelized onion and cheese, and heat in the oven for 5 minutes, or until the cheese is melted. Serve with the reserved cooking liquid for dipping.

Variations:

Make your own garlic bread by using the recipe on page 126. I suggest using a large French baguette and doubling the butter mixture. You can also use any other bread you wish for these sandwiches—I just find them extra delicious with garlic bread!

Fried Chicken Tenders

An insanely popular recipe that comes out perfectly every time. Sliced chicken breasts are coated in a simple batter and fried to golden brown, crispy deliciousness. Serve with Broccoli Rice Casserole (page 99).

Vegetable oil, for frying
2 large chicken breasts, cut against the grain into 1-inch strips
¼ teaspoon garlic powder
¼ teaspoon onion powder
¼ teaspoon paprika
¼ teaspoon seasoned salt
3 cracks black pepper
½ teaspoon baking soda
1 teaspoon baking powder
1 ¼ cups all-purpose flour
1 cup cold water

1. Pour in enough oil to fill a large, deep skillet to about a 1-inch depth and heat over medium heat. Place a wire rack over a baking sheet.

2. Place the chicken in a large bowl and add the garlic powder, onion powder, paprika, seasoned salt, and pepper. Toss to coat. Add the baking soda and baking powder and again toss to coat. Add the flour and coat the chicken evenly. Slowly add the water and mix by hand; the consistency will be similar to that of pancake batter.

3. When the oil is hot, letting any excess batter drip off first, slowly add the chicken pieces, one by one, to the oil. Do not let chicken pieces touch; you will have to fry in batches. Turn the pieces occasionally to get them browned on all sides. The chicken is ready when slightly golden brown and its internal temperature reaches 165°F.

4. Place the chicken on a paper towel–lined plate to soak up the excess oil. Then place the pieces on the prepared wire rack, and continue to fry the remaining chicken.

Spicy Sicilian Chicken Noodle Soup

MAKES
3 TO 4
SERVINGS

A sick day staple, this is a soup I crave regularly, topped with fresh Basil Pesto (page 177) and served with Classic Yeast Rolls (page 123). This is one of those dishes that gets better the next day; I suggest making a double batch! It gets its kick from the black pepper.

1 tablespoon extra virgin olive oil

2 celery stalks, thinly sliced

¾ cup diced carrot

1 cup diced white onion

1 teaspoon kosher salt

15 cracks black pepper

1 plum tomato, cored and diced

1 garlic clove, minced

1 large red potato, scrubbed clean and diced

2 split chicken breasts or ½ chicken

32 ounces chicken stock

6 ounces prepared egg noodles

Basil Pesto (page 177), for garnish (optional)

1. Heat the olive oil in a large saucepan over medium-low heat. Add the celery, carrot, and onion. Season with ½ teaspoon of the salt and 5 cracks of the pepper. Cover and cook, stirring occasionally, until translucent, about 10 minutes.

2. Add the rest of the ingredients, except the noodles and pesto. Bring to a boil, cover, lower the heat to low, and simmer for 3 hours.

3. *Very carefully* remove the chicken from the pot. Discard the bones and skin, shred the meat, and return the meat to the pot. Serve with the noodles and pesto, if desired.

Pro tip:
This recipe calls for bone-in chicken while it cooks. At the end of the recipe, you have to remove the chicken and discard the bones and the skin. Be careful while doing this; the chicken is extremely tender and a few bones might end up in the soup. If you are not confident that you can get all the bones out, I suggest using boneless chicken instead.

Veggie Goat Cheese Frittata

An individual frittata loaded with asparagus, roasted red peppers, and goat cheese. This is a great dish to serve at breakfast, brunch, lunch, or dinner! Made in a small skillet, it can be easily customized to your preference.

1 tablespoon unsalted butter
5 asparagus spears
2 large eggs
Splash of milk
Pinch of kosher salt
2 cracks black pepper
2 tablespoons julienned
   roasted red bell pepper
2 teaspoons thinly sliced chives
2 tablespoons crumbled goat
   cheese
Finely chopped fresh parsley,
   for garnish (optional)

1. Preheat the oven to 400°F.

2. Melt the butter in a 6-inch oven-safe skillet over medium heat. Add the asparagus and cook, turning occasionally, for 5 minutes.

3. While the asparagus is cooking, place the eggs in a small bowl. Add the milk, salt, and black pepper and whisk until frothy.

4. Add the egg mixture to the skillet, followed by the bell pepper and chives. Cook for 3 minutes, or until the sides of the eggs start to set. Add the goat cheese on top. Bake for 5 to 6 minutes, until the eggs are set in the center. Garnish with parsley, if desired.

Pesto Risotto
with Peas

I get on kicks where I make risotto a couple nights a week. It is a creamy, hearty dish that warms my soul. I have to be honest, it does take quite a lot of work. Not hard work, but just lots and lots of stirring. Making your own fresh pesto is just that additional touch to this dish that really makes it shine!

2 cups chicken stock
2 tablespoons unsalted butter
1 garlic clove, minced
½ cup arborio rice
Pinch of kosher salt
3 cracks black pepper
⅓ cup frozen peas
2 tablespoons prepared Basil
   Pesto (page 177)

Note: Set aside some time for this recipe. Pull up a chair, pour yourself a glass of wine, and get ready to stir, stir, stir!

1. Place the stock in a small saucepan and keep warm over medium-low heat.

2. Place 1 tablespoon of the butter and the garlic in a medium sauté pan over medium heat. Cook for 1 minute, or until the butter is melted and the garlic is fragrant. Add the rice and mix to coat with the butter. Season with the salt and pepper.

3. Slowly start to add the stock, ¼ cup at a time, while stirring continuously. Between additions of the stock, you want to cook the rice until almost all the liquid is evaporated, and then add another ¼ cup of stock, stirring the mixture all the while.

4. Keep doing this until all but about ¼ cup of the stock is used. This will take about 30 minutes. The rice should be slightly al dente. Add the remaining stock but don't let it absorb all the way; this will make the rice slightly loose and creamy.

5. Finish with the remaining tablespoon of butter and the peas. Let the peas cook through, about 1 minute. Remove from the heat and add the pesto, stirring to combine. Taste, and adjust the seasoning, if necessary.

On the Side

Rosemary Roasted Fingerling Potatoes

Fingerling potatoes are just special. They are cute but more important, they are extremely delicious. They have a wonderful creaminess to them naturally. They are the perfect potato to roast and serve alongside Brown Sugar Meat Loaf (page 58)!

¾ pound fingerling potatoes, scrubbed clean and cut in half lengthwise

2 ½ teaspoons Rosemary Garlic Olive Oil (page 175) or extra virgin olive oil

½ teaspoon minced fresh rosemary

¼ teaspoon kosher salt

1 crack black pepper

Note: Start by preparing the Rosemary Garlic Olive Oil (page 175), if using.

1. Preheat the oven to 425°F.

2. Place the cut potatoes in a large bowl. Toss with the remaining ingredients. Pour out onto a baking sheet and spread into a single layer. Bake for 30 minutes, turning the potatoes halfway through.

Fried Rice

This is a wonderful dish to make if you happen to have leftover rice sitting in your fridge. You can make it a meal by adding leftover meat to it or loading it up with veggies of your choice. Or serve it how I do, alongside your new favorite dish: Sweet Soy-Glazed Chicken (page 53).

1 cup chicken stock
½ cup long-grain white rice
2 tablespoons unsalted butter
2 large eggs, lightly beaten
¼ cup diced white onion
1 tablespoon soy sauce
½ teaspoon black mushroom
    soy sauce
¼ cup frozen peas

1. Place the chicken stock in a small saucepan. Cover and bring to a boil. Immediately add the rice, cover, and lower the heat to low. Cook for 20 minutes without lifting the lid. After the 20 minutes, remove from the heat and let it continue to steam, covered, for 5 minutes.

2. Heat 1 tablespoon butter in a medium skillet over medium heat and cook the eggs until just set and still a little wet looking. Remove from the pan and set aside.

3. Heat the remaining tablespoon of butter in the pan, add the onion, and cook for 3 minutes. Add the cooked eggs back to the pan along with the rice. Let the rice sit for a few minutes, to form a slight crust. Do this three times, stirring the rice in between. Add the two soy sauces and mix until all the rice is coated. Add the peas and mix—they will warm through very fast—and serve.

Variation:
Use leftover rice, if you have it. Substitute 1½ cups of cooked rice for the uncooked rice and the chicken stock in this recipe. Do everything else the same.

Pro tip: The black mushroom soy sauce in this recipe is what gives the dish its deep brown color. You can find it in any Asian market; even some grocery stores carry it now.

Baked Macaroni and Cheese with Corn Bread Crust

MAKES
3 TO 4
SERVINGS

A twist on a classic, the corn bread crust adds a touch of sweetness to this macaroni and cheese!

¼ pound macaroni pasta

2½ tablespoons unsalted butter, plus more for skillet

1½ tablespoons all-purpose flour

¼ teaspoon paprika

½ teaspoon garlic powder

¼ teaspoon onion powder

1 cup milk

½ cup shredded Colby Jack

1 cup shredded sharp Cheddar

1 cup finely crumbled Honey Corn Bread (page 121; about 1 mini loaf)

1. Cook the macaroni per the directions on the package. Drain and set aside in a large bowl.

2. Meanwhile, preheat the oven to 350°F.

3. Place 1½ tablespoons of the butter and the flour in a medium saucepan over medium heat; whisk to combine. Add the paprika, ¼ teaspoon of the garlic powder, and the onion powder. Cook for 1 minute. Slowly add the milk, stirring constantly to make sure there are no lumps. Cook, stirring constantly, for 3 minutes, or until thickened. Remove from the heat and add all the Colby Jack and ½ cup of the Cheddar. Stir to combine, until the cheese is melted.

4. Pour the cheese sauce over the macaroni and mix to combine. Pour into a greased 8-inch cast-iron skillet or oven-safe dish. Top with the remaining ½ cup of Cheddar.

5. Make the topping by melting the remaining 1 tablespoon of butter in a microwave-safe dish in the microwave for 15 seconds. Add the remaining ¼ teaspoon of garlic powder and the corn bread crumbs. Mix with a spoon to coat the corn bread. Evenly spread the crumb mixture on top of the macaroni. Bake for 25 to 30 minutes, until the top is golden brown and the cheese is bubbly.

Pan-Seared Brussels Sprouts with Bacon

A go-to side dish in our house. We love Brussels sprouts, and your family will, too, after you try this recipe!

3 slices thick-cut bacon, cut into ½-inch dice

12 ounces frozen Brussels sprouts, thawed and cut in half lengthwise

3 cracks black pepper

½ teaspoon salt

⅛ teaspoon garlic powder

1 tablespoon unsalted butter

1. Cook the bacon in a medium skillet over medium-low heat until crispy. Remove the bacon from the pan with a slotted spoon and reserve 1 tablespoon of the bacon grease in the pan.

2. Add the Brussels sprouts to the pan and toss in the fat. Cover and cook, stirring every 2 minutes or so, for 15 minutes.

3. Remove the lid and increase the heat to medium. Continue to cook, stirring occasionally, for 4 minutes, or until the Brussels sprouts are golden brown. Add the pepper, salt, garlic powder, and butter, and toss to coat. Crumble the bacon on top and serve.

Pro tip:
I love using frozen Brussels sprouts for this recipe because they just seem to come out perfect every time! You can use fresh, but keep an eye on them as they may need additional cooking time to become tender.

Broccoli Rice Casserole

This is one of Jeremy's all-time favorite side dishes! The combination of broccoli, rice, and that creamy sauce gets him every time. I suggest serving this with Brown Sugar Meat Loaf (page 58) or Fried Chicken Tenders (page 81).

3 cups water
½ cup long-grain white rice (see note)
Cooking spray
1 cup diced broccoli florets (about 1 crown)
1 tablespoon unsalted butter
1 tablespoon all-purpose flour
⅛ teaspoon garlic powder
⅛ teaspoon onion powder
⅛ teaspoon paprika
½ teaspoon kosher salt
4 cracks black pepper
¾ cup milk
1 tablespoon cream cheese
1 cup shredded sharp Cheddar

Note: Have leftover rice? Skip step 1 and add 1½ cups cooked rice in step 5.

1. Place 1 cup of the water in a small pot over medium-high heat. Cover and bring to a boil. Add the rice and stir to evenly distribute. Cover and reduce heat to low. Cook for 20 minutes. Remove from heat and let stand for 5 minutes.

2. Preheat the oven to 350°F and spray a 5-inch square oven-safe baking dish with cooking spray.

3. Place the broccoli and the remaining 2 cups water in a medium skillet over medium heat, cover, and simmer for 5 minutes. Drain the water and set the broccoli aside.

4. Melt the butter in the same skillet over medium heat. Whisk in the flour, garlic powder, onion powder, paprika, salt, and pepper. Let cook for 1 minute. Add the milk, whisking to make sure there are no lumps. Cook for 5 minutes, or until thickened. Remove from the heat, add the cream cheese, and allow it to melt into the sauce. Add ½ cup of the Cheddar and whisk until melted.

5. Place the cooked rice and broccoli in a large bowl, pour the cream sauce on top, and stir to combine. Pour into the prepared baking dish. Top with the remaining ½ cup of Cheddar. Bake for 25 to 30 minutes, until bubbly.

Rustic Roasted Garlic Mashed Potatoes

I make this potato recipe at least once a week. You can't go wrong with creamy mashed potatoes loaded with roasted garlic. I think a lot of people shy away from making mashed potatoes because they can be time-consuming. Normally, you would have to peel the potatoes, but in this recipe I totally skip that step by using potatoes that have a naturally thin skin.

¾ pound honey gold potatoes, scrubbed and diced
Cold water
¼ cup whole milk
4 tablespoons (½ stick) unsalted butter
2 tablespoons sour cream
¼ teaspoon fresh thyme, minced
¼ teaspoon fresh rosemary, minced
8 cloves Roasted Garlic (page 174), skins removed
½ teaspoon kosher salt
3 cracks black pepper

Notes: Any thin-skinned potato will work for this recipe, including red potatoes, fingerling potatoes, or honey golds as I have used here.

The Roasted Garlic (page 174) should be made ahead of time for this recipe, as it takes 45 minutes to cook.

1. Place the potatoes in a 3-quart saucepan and cover with cold water. Bring to a boil over medium-high heat and boil for 15 minutes, or until soft.

2. While the potatoes are boiling, place the milk and butter in a small saucepan over medium-low heat, to warm through.

3. Drain the potatoes and place back in the cooking pot. Add the warm milk mixture along with the sour cream, herbs, roasted garlic, and salt and pepper. Mash until smooth. Taste and adjust the seasoning if necessary.

Variations:

Mix up this recipe by adding different herbs or bringing in cheese. Try loaded mashed potatoes by adding ½ cup of shredded sharp Cheddar; two strips of bacon, crumbled; and one thinly sliced scallion.

Sweet-and-Sour Red Cabbage

I don't know what it is about cabbage, but I just can't get enough of it! It is a great side dish to many main courses from Marinated Grilled Rib-Eye Steaks (page 49) to Panko Fried Shrimp (page 77). Sweet but tangy and delicious!

2 tablespoons unsalted butter
¼ cup julienned white onion
4 cups diced red cabbage
   (about 1 small head)
⅓ cup cider vinegar
3 tablespoons sugar
⅔ cup water
Pinch of salt

1. Place the butter and onion in a medium saucepan. Cook for 2 minutes over medium heat. Add the cabbage and coat with the butter. Add the remaining ingredients and stir to combine.

2. Bring to a boil, lower the heat to low, cover, and simmer for 45 minutes.

Variations:
Sometimes I like to add two strips of crispy bacon to this as it is cooking, for an extra kick of flavor. I also suggest using bacon fat instead of butter, if you have it on hand.

Baked Potato Wedges

A great accompaniment to any meal, baked potato wedges are especially great alongside Brown Sugar Meat Loaf (page 58), Fish 'N' Chips (page 72), and Grilled Ham and Cheese Sandwiches (page 75)!

2 small russet potatoes,
   scrubbed clean
2 tablespoons olive oil
2 teaspoons seasoned salt
4 cracks black pepper

1. Preheat the oven to 425°F.

2. Cut the potatoes into wedges by cutting in half lengthwise, then cutting in half again lengthwise, so you have four pieces. Then, cut each quarter lengthwise into three parts. Place the potato slices in a bowl and toss with the remaining ingredients.

3. Place the potatoes, in a single layer, on a baking sheet. Bake until golden brown and tender, 30 to 35 minutes, turning once during the cooking process.

Creamy Tangy Potato Salad

Your summer cookout isn't complete without a killer potato salad. My version is simple: just potatoes, celery, and the most amazing dressing ever. Once you taste it, you will be using this dressing as a dipping sauce, sandwich spread, and of course . . . on your everyday salad! I keep a jar in the fridge at all times.

1 pound honey gold potatoes (red potatoes will work, too), washed and scrubbed clean
6 cups cold water
1 celery stalk, diced
1 recipe Garlic Salad Dressing (page 173)
1 scallion, thinly sliced, for garnish (optional)

1. Place the potatoes and water in a large saucepan. Bring to a boil over medium-high heat. Cook until the potatoes are done; they should be easily pierced by a fork all the way through, 20 to 30 minutes. Drain the potatoes and let cool to the touch.

2. When the potatoes are cool, cut into 1-inch dice and place in a large bowl. Add the celery and the dressing. Toss to coat, taste, and adjust the seasoning, if necessary. Cover and chill in the fridge until cold. To serve, garnish with sliced scallion, if using.

Variations:
This is the most basic base recipe there is. Add additional ingredients as desired.

Pro tip:
By using a tender potato like the kind used here, you don't have to peel the potatoes, saving time and energy—score!

Buttered Corn off the Cob

This is one of our favorite side dishes to have in the summer months when the stores are overflowing with fresh corn! Buttery, sweet goodness!

Kernels sliced off 2 ears of corn (about 1 ½ cups)
¼ teaspoon kosher salt
½ teaspoon finely chopped fresh parsley (optional)

1. Melt the butter in a small skillet over medium heat. Add the corn and season with the salt. Toss the skillet or stir occasionally for 5 minutes.

2. Serve garnished with parsley, if desired.

Cheesy Skillet Potatoes

Need a super easy potato side dish? Cheesy Skillet Potatoes to the rescue: thinly sliced potatoes that don't need to be peeled, fried up in bacon fat and topped with Cheddar, a simple, quick, and sinfully delicious side!

1 tablespoon bacon fat or
  butter
1 russet potato, scrubbed
  clean and thinly sliced on a
  mandoline at the thinnest
  setting
1 teaspoon garlic powder
1 teaspoon kosher salt
Freshly cracked pepper
1 cup shredded sharp Cheddar

1. Melt the bacon fat in a medium skillet over medium heat. Place about a quarter of the potato slices, in a single, slightly overlapping layer, in the skillet. Season with some of the garlic powder, salt, and a crack of pepper. Continue layering the potatoes and seasoning until all the potatoes are used up. There will be about four layers total.

2. Cover and let cook undisturbed for 10 minutes. Carefully flip the potatoes with a spatula and press the top of the potatoes back into the pan, to form a golden crust. Continue to cook the potatoes, flipping them every few minutes, getting them as brown as possible on all sides.

3. When the potatoes are cooked through and browned, about 10 more minutes, remove from the heat and top with the cheese.

Grilled Asparagus

Asparagus is a favorite vegetable at our house. Grilling asparagus just adds a whole other dimension of flavor. My favorite, favorite way to make this is over charcoal. There is nothing like that smoke from coal that adds an extra pop! Anytime we are cooking something over the coals, I automatically make asparagus alongside it. It's an obsession, I know.

1 pound asparagus
2 teaspoons extra virgin olive
 oil
2 cracks black pepper
¼ teaspoon kosher salt
⅛ teaspoon garlic powder

Pro tip:
Blanching allows the asparagus to cook halfway through, so it doesn't have to stay on the grill for too long. I have noticed if you place the asparagus on the grill raw, it can dry out easily. Following the method in this recipe, you have juicy, vibrant green asparagus every time! I love it when asparagus is extra tender, but if you like a crisper vegetable, I suggest cooking it on the grill for half the recommended time.

1. Rinse the asparagus thoroughly, then trim off the woody ends, about 2 inches of the way up.

2. Fill a 3-quart saucepan halfway with water. Bring to a boil, lower the heat to a simmer (medium-low), add the asparagus, and cook for 4 minutes. Drain. If you are not planning to grill the asparagus immediately, now is the time to shock it in ice water; see pro tip below.

3. Transfer to a plate and season with the remaining ingredients, tossing to make sure the asparagus is coated.

4. Prepare the grill. Grill over medium heat until tender, 5 to 8 minutes.

This can be a make-ahead recipe, which I use quite often: Prepare the asparagus per steps 1 and 2. After draining, shock in an ice-water bath (1 quart water, 1 quart ice) to stop the cooking process, drain, and set aside until ready to proceed. The blanched asparagus can be stored in the refrigerator for up to 1 day before grilling.

The BEST Collard Greens

If you are from the South, collard greens have definitely come across your table a time or two. I've been told by more than a handful of people that this recipe is by far the best collards they have ever tasted. Try it out for yourself!

1 ham hock
32 ounces chicken stock
1 tablespoon onion powder
1 tablespoon garlic powder
1 head collard greens, stripped, washed, and cut into ½-inch strips
1 teaspoon seasoned salt
2 cracks black pepper
1 tablespoon unsalted butter

1. Sear the ham hock on all sides in a medium saucepan over medium-high heat until golden brown. Add the chicken stock, onion powder, and garlic powder. Bring to a boil, cover, lower the heat to low, and simmer for 2 hours.

2. Remove the ham hock, allow to cool to the touch, and set aside.

3. Add the collards to the pot, a handful at a time, and wilt them down. Season with the seasoned salt and pepper, cover, and cook for 2 more hours, or until the desired tenderness is achieved. Pick all the meat off the ham hock and add it to the pot at any time.

4. Just before serving, add the butter and stir to combine.

Variation

You can also make these greens in a slow cooker. After searing the ham hock, proceed with step 1, using a slow cooker instead of a saucepan. Cook on high for 2 hours or on low for 4 hours. In step 3, add the collards to the slow cooker and cook for an additional hour on high or 2 hours on low. Complete recipe as directed.

Hasselback Sweet Potatoes

"Hasselbacking" seems to be all the rage at the moment. What I like about it is that it helps cook your food more evenly. This way whatever you are cooking gets a crispy edge with a perfectly cooked interior. Plus, it is the perfect vehicle for toppings, and that's right up my alley! This recipe would be the perfect alternative to making a sweet potato casserole during the holidays.

2 medium sweet potatoes, scrubbed clean
2 tablespoons unsalted butter
¼ teaspoon kosher salt
1 tablespoon packed light brown sugar
2 tablespoons chopped pecans
Handful of mini marshmallows

1. Preheat the oven to 425°F.

2. Slice the potatoes widthwise ⅛ inch thick along the whole potato, stopping about ¼ inch from the bottom edge so that they are not cut all the way through. To do this, I place two wooden spoon handles alongside the potatoes to stop the knife. Place the potatoes on a baking sheet.

3. Melt 1 tablespoon of the butter and mix with the salt; drizzle this on top of the potatoes. Bake for 40 minutes; halfway through, take a fork and gently separate the slices so they fan out.

4. Mix the remaining tablespoon of butter with the brown sugar and brush this on top of the potatoes as evenly as possible, trying to get it down between the slices. Top with the pecans and marshmallows. You will have to try your best to balance the marshmallows on top. Bake for another 3 minutes, just until the marshmallows turn golden.

Stovetop Green Beans with Bacon

Once you taste this recipe for green beans, you will think they were slow cooked for hours. Intensely flavorful beans in a smoky bacon sauce, they are out of this world delicious.

2 slices thick-cut bacon, cut into ½-inch dice

1 pound green beans, stems removed

1½ teaspoons seasoned salt

¼ teaspoon garlic powder

¼ teaspoon onion powder

4 cracks black pepper

1 tablespoon tomato paste

¼ cup chicken stock

1. Cook the bacon in a medium skillet over medium-low heat until crispy. Remove the bacon from the pan and drain on paper towels, reserving 1 tablespoon of the bacon fat in the pan.

2. Increase the heat to medium-high. Add the green beans and blister the skin, stirring constantly, for 5 minutes.

3. Lower the heat to medium-low and add the remaining ingredients to the pan, including the cooked bacon. Cover and simmer for 10 minutes, or until the beans are fork-tender.

Mini Honey Corn Bread Loaves

Who doesn't love corn bread? In individual loaves and sweetened with honey, these are an extra-special treat for any meal! This recipe doubles as a topping for Baked Macaroni and Cheese with Corn Bread Crust (page 95)—it adds a sweet crunch that really makes the baked pasta pop!

Cooking spray
½ cup cornmeal
6 tablespoons all-purpose flour
¾ teaspoon baking powder
¼ teaspoon baking soda
⅛ teaspoon kosher salt
3 tablespoons unsalted butter,
    melted and cooled
1 large egg
6 tablespoons sour cream
6 tablespoons milk
3 tablespoons honey

1. Preheat the oven to 425°F. Spray four sections of a mini loaf pan or four individual mini loaf pans with cooking spray; set aside.

2. Mix together the cornmeal, flour, baking powder, baking soda, and salt in a medium bowl.

3. Whisk together butter, egg, sour cream, milk, and 2 tablespoons of the honey in a separate medium bowl. Fold in the flour mixture.

4. Divide the batter among the prepared mini loaf pan sections or pans. Drizzle with the remaining tablespoon of honey. Bake for 12 to 15 minutes, until golden brown along the edges; a toothpick inserted into the center of a loaf should come out clean. Let cool for 5 minutes in the pan, then transfer to a wire rack to cool completely.

Classic Yeast Rolls

*Light and airy yeast rolls are the perfect addition to any dinner!
I love to have them as a snack with some butter and Strawberry
Jam (page 151)—yum!*

1 tablespoon unsalted butter,
   melted and cooled to room
   temperature
1 ½ teaspoons sugar
½ cup warm water, 120° to 130°F
1 ⅛ teaspoons rapid-rise yeast
1 large egg, lightly beaten
½ teaspoon kosher salt
1 ¼ cups all-purpose flour
Cooking spray

1. Combine the melted butter, sugar, water, and yeast in a large bowl and stir well. Wait 3 to 5 minutes, until bubbles form. Add half of the beaten egg, plus the salt and the flour. Stir well with a spoon. Place a clean towel on top of the bowl and let sit for 45 minutes, until the dough doubles in size.

2. Meanwhile, preheat the oven to 425°F. Spray four sections of a mini loaf pan or four individual mini loaf pans with cooking spray.

3. Divide the dough into four equal portions and dollop into the prepared pan sections or pans—using an ice-cream scoop here really helps. The dough will be very sticky and looks like it needs more flour, but it doesn't! Let rise for an additional 10 minutes in the pan.

4. Brush the tops of the rolls with the remaining egg. Bake for 10 to 12 minutes, until lightly golden brown. Let cool for 5 minutes in the pan, then remove from the pan and allow to cool completely on a wire rack.

Pro tip:
Be extra aware while making this recipe: When using yeast, you want to make sure the warm water does not go above 130°F.

Cheesy Pesto Pull-Apart Rolls

Using the recipe for Classic Yeast Rolls (previous page), fresh Basil Pesto (page 177), and mozzarella, these rolls will be the hit of any meal! Made in a muffin tin, they look pretty cute, too!

1 recipe Classic Yeast Roll
   dough (page 123)
Cooking spray
2 tablespoons Basil Pesto (page
   177)
½ cup shredded mozzarella

1. Prepare the Classic Yeast Roll recipe (page 123) through step 1.

2. Preheat the oven to 425°F. Spray four cups of a muffin tin with cooking spray.

3. In the prepared muffin tin, using a 1-tablespoon scooper, dollop one scoop of dough into the bottom of each muffin cup. Brush with pesto and add a pinch of cheese. Keep doing this among the four muffin cups until all the dough is used. Make sure the top of each roll is brushed with pesto; add a last sprinkling of cheese.

4. Bake for 10 to 15 minutes, until golden brown, let cool for 5 minutes in the tin, then transfer to a wire rack to cool completely.

Ciabatta Garlic Bread

We all need a good, quick garlic bread recipe up our sleeve. Ciabatta is one of my favorite types of bread, but feel free to use whatever style rolls you like for this recipe.

1 garlic clove, minced
2 tablespoons unsalted butter
3 tablespoons freshly grated
    Parmigiano-Reggiano
1 tablespoon finely chopped
    fresh parsley
Pinch of kosher salt
2 ciabatta rolls, cut in half
    lengthwise

1. Preheat the oven to 350°F.

2. Place the garlic and butter in a small saucepan over medium heat and cook until fragrant, 3 minutes.

3. Mix the cheese, parsley, and salt with the butter. Brush this mixture all over the rolls, concentrating on the cut portion. Bake for 10 minutes.

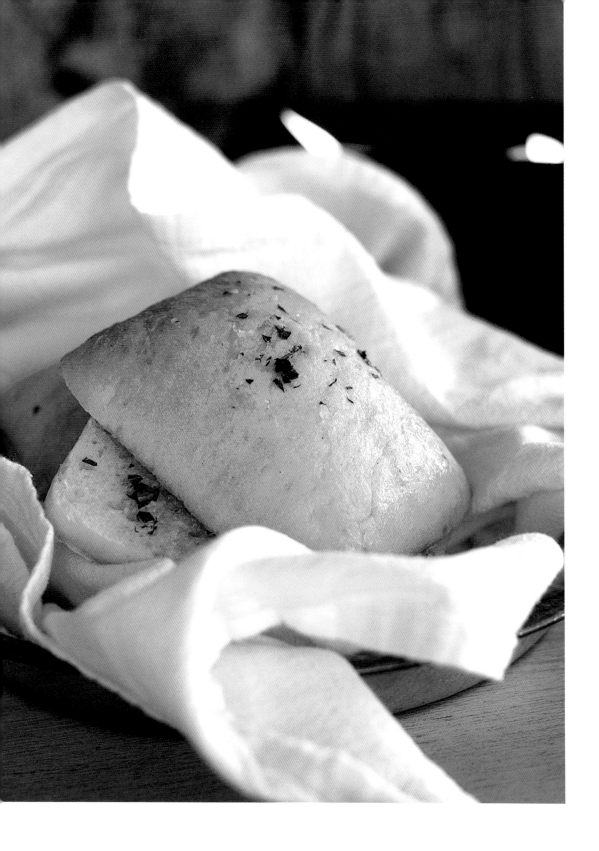

Cream Cheese Biscuits

The most flavorful biscuits you will ever make—and eat! These come together and bake in just 15 minutes. Talk about easy.

½ cup all-purpose flour, plus more for dusting
¾ teaspoon baking powder
Pinch of kosher salt
2 tablespoons unsalted butter
¾ ounce cream cheese
2 tablespoons plus 2 teaspoons milk

1. Preheat the oven to 450°F.

2. Whisk together the flour, baking powder, and salt in a medium bowl. Cut in 1 tablespoon of the butter and all of the cream cheese. Make a well in the center and add the milk, mixing with a spoon until it just comes together.

3. Turn out the mixture onto a floured surface and knead a few times, just until a dough forms. Roughly form it into a square and, using a rolling pin, roll it out to ½ inch thick. Cut into fourths. Place the biscuits 2 inches apart on a baking sheet.

4. Melt the remaining tablespoon of butter and brush on top of the biscuits. Bake for 10 to 12 minutes, until slightly golden brown.

Sweets 'N' Treats

Fried Apple Crumble

My favorite desserts are ones where there is a hot and cold element to them. This recipe would be the hot element of one of our most loved fall desserts, along with a scoop of No-Churn Vanilla Bean Ice Cream (following page). We are in heaven!

For the filling
2 Granny Smith apples, peeled
4 tablespoons (½ stick)
    unsalted butter
¼ cup packed light brown sugar
1 ½ teaspoons ground
    cinnamon
½ teaspoon vanilla bean paste
No-Churn Vanilla Bean Ice
    Cream (page 134), for serving
    (optional)

For the crumble topping
¼ cup packed light brown sugar
¼ cup all-purpose flour
1 tablespoon unsalted butter
Pinch of salt

Make the filling:

1. Cut the apples into slices by cutting them first in half, and then into quarters. Remove the stems and seeds. Cut each quarter into three pieces lengthwise.

2. Preheat the oven to 400°F.

3. Heat the butter in a large skillet over medium heat. Add the brown sugar and cinnamon. Stir until the sugar is melted, add the apples and vanilla bean paste. Cook, stirring occasionally, for 10 to 15 minutes, until the apples are fork-tender. Pour everything into an 8-inch baking pan.

Prepare the crumble topping:

1. Place all the topping ingredients in a bowl and roll between your fingers until the mixture has a consistency similar to sand. Pour the mixture over the apples. (This will look like too much, but it isn't; use all of it.)

2. Bake for 20 to 25 minutes, until golden brown and bubbly. Serve with vanilla ice cream, if desired.

No-Churn Vanilla Bean Ice Cream

A simple ice cream that comes together in minutes. Using a good-quality vanilla bean paste makes this cold treat extra special. Pair it with Fried Apple Crumble (previous page) and you have one of our all-time favorite fall desserts!

1 cup heavy cream
7 ounces sweetened
   condensed milk
1 teaspoon vanilla bean paste

1. Place the cream in a large bowl; metal is best if you have it. Whip the cream, using an electric mixer on medium speed, until soft peaks form. Add the milk and vanilla and whip just to combine.

2. Cover and freeze for 6 hours or overnight.

Variations:
This is the most basic of base recipes. Go wild: add fresh strawberries, candy pieces, or chopped sandwich cookies!

Strawberry Shortcakes

I remember the first time I had a "proper" strawberry shortcake. I was around six or seven and my northern grandma made them for us. I was in love instantly! A sweet biscuit topped with macerated berries and heaps of homemade whipped cream . . . it doesn't get much better than this!

For the berries
2 cups hulled and quartered
   strawberries
1 tablespoon granulated sugar

For the shortbread
1 tablespoon plus ½ teaspoon
   granulated sugar
1 cup all-purpose flour
1 teaspoon baking powder
⅛ teaspoon baking soda
Pinch of salt
¾ cup heavy cream
½ teaspoon pure vanilla extract

**For the vanilla bean whipped
cream**
1 cup heavy cream
2 tablespoons powdered sugar
½ teaspoon vanilla bean paste

Note: The strawberries need at least an hour to macerate.

Prepare the berries:

1. Mix the strawberries with the granulated sugar, cover with plastic wrap, and chill in the refrigerator for 1 hour, up to overnight.

Make the shortbread:

1. Preheat the oven to 400°F.

2. Sift together the tablespoon of granulated sugar, flour, baking powder, baking soda, and salt into a large bowl. Add the cream and vanilla and stir with a spoon until just combined.

3. Make two drop biscuits by dividing the dough in two and placing each portion freeform on an ungreased cookie sheet. Sprinkle with the remaining ½ teaspoon of granulated sugar. Bake for 18 to 20 minutes, until lightly golden brown. Transfer to a wire rack and let cool completely.

Make the whipped cream:

1. Just before serving, place the cream in a large bowl, preferably metal. Using an electric mixer, mix on high speed until soft peaks form. Add the powdered sugar and vanilla. Whip until all the ingredients are combined and the cream is whipped into medium peaks.

2. To serve, cut the biscuits in half and add a dollop of the whipped cream and about half of the strawberries to the bottom halves. Top with other half of each biscuit and garnish with more whipped cream and berries.

Banana Pudding Parfait with Homemade Vanilla Wafers

Banana pudding has always held a place in my heart. It is one of my favorite desserts that my grandma made, of course prepared in the traditional southern way with vanilla wafers and meringue. I put a twist on this dessert by assembling homemade wafers, pudding, fresh bananas, and homemade whipped cream in a cute little parfait!

For the vanilla pudding

¼ cup sugar
1 tablespoon cornstarch
Pinch of kosher salt
1½ cups milk
2 large egg yolks
2 tablespoons unsalted butter
1 teaspoon vanilla bean paste

For the vanilla wafers

4 tablespoons (½ stick) unsalted butter, at room temperature
½ cup sugar
1 large egg yolk
1½ teaspoons vanilla bean paste
½ cup plus 3 tablespoons all-purpose flour
¼ plus ⅛ teaspoon baking powder
Pinch of kosher salt

Note: You will have to make the vanilla pudding and vanilla wafers ahead of time for this recipe.

Make the vanilla pudding:

1. Place the sugar, cornstarch, salt, milk, and egg in a small saucepan and whisk to combine. Place over medium heat and cook, stirring constantly, until the mixture starts to simmer. Lower the heat to medium-low and cook, continuing to whisk, until the mixture is thickened and you can make ribbons in the pudding, 3 to 5 minutes.

2. Remove from the heat, strain through a mesh strainer, and add the butter and vanilla. Immediately place plastic wrap on top and chill in the refrigerator for 2 hours.

Make the vanilla wafers:

1. Place the butter and sugar in a medium bowl and cream until fluffy, using an electric mixer, about 2 minutes. Add the egg and vanilla and beat until smooth. Mix together the flour, salt, and baking powder in a separate bowl. Add to the butter mixture and mix until combined. Cover with plastic wrap and chill in the refrigerator for 10 minutes.

2. While the dough is chilling, preheat the oven to 350°F.

3. Roll the dough into teaspoon-size balls and place about 1½ inches apart on an ungreased

For the assembly

1 recipe Vanilla Bean Whipped
Cream (page 137)
1 medium-size banana, thinly
sliced

cookie sheet. Bake for 12 to 15 minutes, until the
edges are slightly golden brown. Transfer to
a wire rack to cool completely. Makes 18 to 20
cookies.

Assemble the parfaits:

1. Chop up a few cookies and place in the
bottom of two small glasses. Pour one-quarter
of the pudding into each glass and top with a
layer of whipped cream. Add a layer of sliced
banana and repeat. Garnish with cookie crumbs
and banana slices, and serve immediately.

Pro tip: Feel free to make the cake in advance and frost the next day!

Chocolate Malt Layer Cake

If you are a chocoholic like me, then you will really appreciate this cake: a 6-inch double-layer chocolate cake with chocolate malt frosting, dripping chocolate ganache and garnished with malted milk balls. A chocolate lover's dream! This cake is much smaller than a traditional layer cake, perfect for serving two to three people.

For the cake

Cooking spray

½ cup cake flour

2 tablespoons plus 2 teaspoons unsweetened cocoa powder

¼ teaspoon baking powder

⅛ teaspoon baking soda

Pinch of kosher salt

1 tablespoon malted milk powder

¼ cup sour cream

¼ cup whole milk

6 tablespoons granulated sugar

2½ tablespoons unsalted butter, melted and cooled

½ teaspoon vanilla bean paste or pure vanilla extract

For the chocolate malt frosting

8 teaspoons (1 stick) unsalted butter, at room temperature

1 teaspoon vanilla bean paste or pure vanilla extract

3½ cups powdered sugar

½ cup unsweetened cocoa powder

½ cup malted milk powder

Pinch of kosher salt

5 tablespoons whole milk

Make the cake:

1. Preheat the oven to 350°F. Grease a 6-inch round cake pan with cooking spray.

2. Whisk together the flour, cocoa powder, baking powder, baking soda, salt, and malted milk powder in a medium bowl. Set aside.

3. Place the sour cream, milk, granulated sugar, melted butter, and vanilla in a large bowl and whisk together, then slowly add the flour mixture and whisk until there are no lumps. Pour the mixture into the prepared cake pan. Bake for 30 to 34 minutes, until a toothpick inserted into the center comes out clean. Let cool completely on a wire rack.

Make the chocolate malt frosting:

1. Place the butter in a medium bowl and cream until fluffy, using an electric mixer, for 1 minute. Add the vanilla and beat to combine.

2. Whisk together the powdered sugar, cocoa powder, and malted milk powder in a separate bowl. Slowly add to the butter mixture, alternating with the whole milk. The mixture will be light and fluffy.

continued

For the chocolate ganache

¼ cup heavy cream

6 tablespoons milk chocolate chips

Malted milk balls, for garnish (optional)

Make the chocolate ganache:

1. Place the chocolate chips into a small, heat-proof bowl. Heat the cream until boiling in a small pot, then pour over chocolate chips. Mix with a spoon until smooth. Let cool.

Assemble the cake:

1. Cut the cooled cake in half lengthwise. Place a layer of frosting on top and smooth with a spatula. Place the other layer on top. Spread a very thin layer of frosting all around the side of the cake. Place in the refrigerator and chill for 30 minutes.

2. Frost the cake and pour the cooled ganache on top, allowing it to drizzle down the sides. Garnish with malted milk balls, if desired.

Marble Cookies and Cream Truffles

MAKES
3 TO 4
SERVINGS

An addictive bite-size treat. Sandwich cookies are made into truffles with the addition of cream cheese and marbled for a pretty presentation!

8 golden Oreos, or similar cookies

8 classic Oreos, or similar cookies

4 ounces cream cheese, softened

8 ounces milk chocolate chips

1. Line a baking sheet with parchment paper or a silicone mat.

2. Place the golden Oreos in a food processor and process into crumbs. Add half of the cream cheese and process until smooth. Place the mixture in a small bowl and set aside.

3. Repeat with the regular Oreos.

4. Using a 1-tablespoon scoop (or eyeball 1 tablespoon's worth of filling), scoop and press together small chunks of both mixtures to form the marbled look. Roll into a ball and set aside on the prepared baking sheet. Repeat until all the mixture is used.

5. Freeze until frozen solid, 4 hours, up to overnight.

6. Melt your chocolate the easy way: Place the chocolate in a microwave-safe bowl. Microwave for 15-second intervals on medium power. Stir between each interval until just melted.

7. Dip the truffles in the melted chocolate until coated and place back on the prepared baking sheet. Immediately decorate with leftover cookie crumbles, if desired. Let the outer shell harden before serving.

Jumbo Chocolate Chip Cookies

These chocolate chip cookies are the ultimate, bakery style and about the size of your hand. You could share but . . . do you really want to? I thought so! Crunchy around the edges, soft, chewy, and gooey on the inside, this is a cookie for everyone!

4 tablespoons (½ stick) unsalted butter, at room temperature
¼ cup granulated sugar
2 tablespoons packed light brown sugar
1 large egg
½ teaspoon vanilla bean paste
¾ cup all-purpose flour
¼ teaspoon baking soda
Pinch of kosher salt
½ cup milk chocolate chips (or chocolate chip of your preference)

1. Cream together the butter and sugars in a medium bowl, using an electric mixer, for 1 minute. Add the egg and vanilla; beat to combine. Mix together the flour, baking soda, and salt in a separate bowl. Gradually add to the butter mixture and stir. Fold in the chocolate chips.

2. Cover and place in the refrigerator for 1 hour.

3. Meanwhile, preheat the oven to 350°F.

4. Divide the dough into two equal portions. Roll one portion into a large ball, place on a cookie sheet, and gently press down just a little bit so the top is flat. Repeat with the other portion of the dough, leaving 4 inches between the two cookies. Bake for 18 to 20 minutes until golden brown along the edges and the center looks dry and no longer moist.

5. Remove from the oven and let sit on the cookie sheet, on a heat-safe surface, for at least 10 minutes to continue cooking. Transfer to a wire rack to cool completely.

Pro tip: To ensure your chocolate chips don't sink to the bottom of the banana bread batter, toss them in flour before folding them in!

Mini White Chocolate Cheesecake-Filled Banana Bread Loaves

Banana bread, cheesecake, white chocolate . . . in mini loaf form. Breakfast? Dessert? Snack? You be the judge. All I know is, dang, these are delicious!

For the banana bread

½ cup mashed banana (1 small banana)
2 tablespoons unsalted butter, melted
¼ teaspoon pure vanilla extract
2 tablespoons packed light brown sugar
1 large egg, lightly beaten
2 tablespoons sour cream
½ cup all-purpose flour
¼ teaspoon baking soda
Pinch of kosher salt
2 tablespoons white chocolate chips

For the filling

2 ounces cream cheese, softened
¼ cup white chocolate chips, melted
¼ teaspoon pure vanilla extract
½ teaspoon all-purpose flour
1 tablespoon granulated sugar

For the glaze

¼ cup powdered sugar
1 teaspoon milk

Make the bread:

1. Preheat the oven to 375°F. Grease three sections of a mini loaf tin or three individual mini loaf pans; set aside.

2. Place the banana, butter, vanilla, brown sugar, half of the beaten egg, and the sour cream in a medium bowl. Whisk to combine. Mix together the flour, baking soda, and salt in a separate bowl. Reserving about 1 tablespoon of the flour mixture, fold the flour into the butter. Toss the chocolate chips in the reserved flour and then fold into the batter. Divide half of the batter among the three mini loaf tin sections or pans. Set aside the remaining half of the batter.

Make the filling:

1. Cream the cream cheese in a medium bowl, using an electric mixer. Add the remaining filling ingredients and beat until well mixed. Dollop this mixture equally among the three loaves. Top equally with the reserved banana bread batter.

2. Bake for 25 to 30 minutes, until a toothpick inserted into the center of a loaf comes out mostly clean. Cool for 10 minutes in the pan on a wire rack. Remove from the pans and cool completely.

Make the glaze:

1. Whisk the powdered sugar and milk together in a small bowl or cup. Pour evenly over the loaves.

Small-Batch Chocolate Peanut Butter Fudge

This no-cook fudge recipe couldn't be any easier! With its classic flavor combo of chocolate and peanut butter, you will get rave reviews for this fudge.

4 ounces cream cheese, softened
2 cups powdered sugar
½ teaspoon pure vanilla extract
¼ cup smooth peanut butter
1 cup milk chocolate chips, melted

1. Cream together the cream cheese and sugar in a medium bowl, using an electric mixer. Add the vanilla.

2. Place the peanut butter in a separate medium, microwaveable bowl and microwave for 20 seconds on half power. Add one-third of the cream cheese mixture to the peanut butter, mix to combine, and set aside.

3. Add the melted chocolate to the cream cheese mixture and mix to combine.

4. Line a 5-inch baking dish with plastic wrap. Press half of the chocolate mixture into the bottom of the dish. Spread the peanut butter mixture on top. Top with the rest of the chocolate mixture. Refrigerate for 4 hours, or until set.

Strawberry Cheesecake Bars

Graham cracker crust, strawberry jam, and rich cheesecake all in a handheld bar . . . perfection!

For the strawberry jam
1 cup hulled and diced
   strawberries
2 teaspoons water
2 teaspoons sugar
Cornstarch slurry (½ teaspoon
   cornstarch mixed with
   1 tablespoon water)

For the crust
1 ½ tablespoons unsalted
   butter, melted
½ cup Graham Cracker (page
   167) crumbs

For the cheesecake
4 ounces cream cheese,
   softened
2 tablespoons plus 2 teaspoons
   sugar
2 tablespoons plus 2 teaspoons
   sour cream
¼ teaspoon pure vanilla extract
1 large egg yolk

Note: The strawberry jam
takes about 10 minutes to
make, so I suggest making
that first. Use the leftovers
on Peanut Butter and Jelly
Blondies (page 155) or on
top of Cream Cheese Biscuits
(page 129)!

Make the jam:

1. Place the strawberries, water, and sugar in a small saucepan over medium-low heat. Bring to a boil, cover, and lower the heat to low. Simmer, stirring occasionally, for 10 minutes. Whisk in the cornstarch slurry and simmer for 2 more minutes. Remove from the heat and let cool.

Make the crust:

1. Preheat the oven to 325°F.

2. Mix the melted butter with the graham cracker crumbs and press the mixture into the prepared baking dish. Set aside.

Make the cheesecake:

1. Cream together the cream cheese and sugar in a medium bowl, using an electric mixer, until smooth. Add the remaining cheesecake ingredients and mix to combine. Pour over the graham cracker crust.

2. Spread 2 tablespoons of the jam on top of the cheesecake mixture. Bake for 30 minutes, or until the cheesecake is the slightest bit jiggly. Let cool slightly, cover with plastic wrap, and chill in the refrigerator for 2 hours.

German Chocolate Brownie Bites

What is it about German chocolate desserts that everyone loves? I think it's that unique frosting. Coconut and pecans all in a luscious caramel sauce—yum! Instead of a huge cake, I made German Chocolate Brownies Bites; could they be any cuter?

For the brownies
Cooking spray
3 ounces German chocolate
2 tablespoons unsalted butter
¼ cup plus 1 tablespoon
    all-purpose flour
¼ cup sugar
½ teaspoon pure vanilla extract
⅛ teaspoon baking powder
Pinch of salt
1 large egg yolk, lightly beaten

For the frosting
⅓ cup sugar
⅓ cup evaporated milk
2 tablespoons plus 2 teaspoons
    unsalted butter
1 large egg yolk, lightly beaten
⅓ cup shredded sweetened
    coconut
⅓ cup chopped pecans
¼ teaspoon pure vanilla extract

Make the brownies:

1. Preheat the oven to 350°F. Grease 14 compartments of a mini muffin tin with cooking spray.

2. Place the chocolate and butter in a small saucepan over low heat and melt, stirring constantly. Remove from the heat and stir in the remaining brownie ingredients.

3. Fill each compartment of the prepared mini muffin tin half full with the brownie dough. Bake for 10 to 12 minutes, until a toothpick inserted in the center of a brownie comes out almost clean. Immediately, using an object that is small and round, such as the end of a wooden spoon, make an indentation in the middle of all the baked brownies. Let cool completely on a wire rack.

Make the frosting:

1. While the brownies are cooling, combine all the frosting ingredients in a small saucepan over low heat. Cook, stirring constantly, until thickened, about 10 minutes. Let cool slightly, then fill the brownies with the frosting.

Peanut Butter and Jelly Blondies

The classic flavor combo made into a sinful dessert, these blondies are loaded with peanut butter flavor and topped with a fresh cherry sauce. Feel free to use Cherry Sauce (page 157) or Strawberry Jam (page 151); either way, these are amazing!

¼ cup smooth peanut butter
2 tablespoons unsalted butter
½ cup packed light brown sugar
1 large egg
¼ teaspoon vanilla bean paste
¼ cup plus 2 tablespoons all-purpose flour
¼ cup Cherry Sauce (page 157) or Strawberry Jam (page 151)

Note: Yes, this cooking time seems extra long, and it is. It takes a while for this blondie to set properly, but don't worry, covering it with the foil helps make sure these stay nice and chewy and not overdone!

1. Preheat the oven to 350°F. Line a 5-inch baking pan with foil or parchment paper and set aside.

2. Place the peanut butter and butter in a medium, microwave-safe bowl. Microwave for 20 seconds on half power, add the brown sugar, and whisk to combine. Add the egg and vanilla; whisk to combine. Fold in the flour until there are no dry lumps. Pour into the prepared dish. Top with the cherry sauce.

3. Bake for 20 minutes, cover with foil, and bake for an additional 40 minutes. Remove from the oven and let cool before serving.

Marble Cheesecake Cupcakes with Cherry Sauce

Sometimes you just can't decide between chocolate and vanilla. I solved that problem with these marble cheesecake cupcakes! Nothing goes better with chocolate or cheesecake, in my opinion, than a luscious fresh cherry sauce. Don't like cherries? Top it off with fresh Strawberry Jam (page 151)!

For the crust
½ cup Graham Cracker (page 167) crumbs
1½ tablespoons unsalted butter, melted
1½ teaspoons packed light brown sugar

For the filling
8 ounces cream cheese, softened
1 large egg
1 tablespoon sour cream
½ cup granulated sugar
2¼ teaspoons all-purpose flour
¼ teaspoon vanilla bean paste
3 tablespoons milk chocolate chips, melted

Make the crust:

1. Preheat the oven to 350°F. Line six cups of a muffin tin with paper liners; set aside.

2. Mix together all the crust ingredients and divide equally among the prepared muffin cups. Press the crust into the liners.

Make the filling:

1. Beat the cream cheese in a medium bowl, using an electric mixer, until smooth. Add the egg and sour cream and whip until smooth. Add the granulated sugar, flour, and vanilla and whip to combine. Place one-quarter of this mixture in a separate small bowl, add the melted chocolate, and mix together.

2. Drop teaspoon-size dollops of each mixture over the graham cracker crusts. Do this until the two cheesecake mixtures are used up. Bake for 18 to 23 minutes, until the cheesecakes are just the slightest bit jiggly. Remove from the oven and let cool in the tin for 5 minutes, then remove the cupcakes and cool completely on a wire rack. Chill in the fridge for at least 1 hour, or until cold; serve with cherry sauce.

For the cherry sauce

1 pound fresh cherries, stemmed and pitted
1 teaspoon fresh lemon juice
1 tablespoon cornstarch
¼ cup granulated sugar
¼ teaspoon pure vanilla extract
Pinch of salt

Make the cherry sauce:

1. Place the cherries in a small saucepan. Mix the lemon juice with the cornstarch in a small cup or bowl, until smooth, then add to the cherries along with the remaining sauce ingredients. Cook over medium heat for 5 to 10 minutes, until thickened. Remove from the heat and let cool. Store in an airtight container in the refrigerator.

Baked Chocolate Chip Donut Holes

Need an easy breakfast treat in a hurry? Donut holes to the rescue! These donut holes are loaded with chocolate chips, baked in a mini muffin tin, and dipped in vanilla glaze—yum!

For the donut holes
Cooking spray
¾ cup all-purpose flour
¾ teaspoon baking powder
Pinch of kosher salt
1 tablespoon unsalted butter, melted and cooled
1 large egg, lightly beaten
1 teaspoon vanilla bean paste
¼ cup granulated sugar
¼ cup milk
¼ cup milk chocolate chips

For the vanilla glaze
1¾ cups powdered sugar
1 teaspoon pure vanilla extract
¼ cup milk

Make the donut holes:

1. Preheat the oven to 350°F. Grease a mini muffin tin.

2. Mix together the flour with the baking powder and salt in a medium bowl.

3. Mix together the butter, egg, and vanilla in a separate medium bowl. Whisk in the granulated sugar and milk until combined. Add the flour mixture and mix until there are no lumps. Fold in the chocolate chips

4. Fill the compartments of the prepared mini muffin tin half full. Bake for 6 to 7 minutes, until a toothpick inserted into the center of a donut hole comes out clean. Transfer to a wire rack to cool.

Make the vanilla glaze:

1. Whisk all the glaze ingredients together in a small bowl until smooth. Dip each donut hole into the glaze and place back on the wire rack. Dip each donut hole again, and serve.

Mini Lemon Meringue Pies

A great little treat for a midday pick-me-up. Zesty lemon curd in crunch phyllo cups topped with fluffy meringue—doesn't this just scream "summer"?

1 large egg
⅓ cup sugar
1 tablespoon lemon zest
1½ tablespoons fresh lemon juice
⅓ cup water
2 teaspoons cornstarch
2 teaspoons all-purpose flour
1 teaspoon unsalted butter
12 phyllo shells

1. Preheat the oven to 350°F.

2. Separate the egg. Place the yolk in a small bowl and put the white in a medium bowl. Place the egg white in the refrigerator for later use.

3. Mix the egg yolk with 3 tablespoons of the sugar; set aside.

4. Place the lemon zest and juice, water, cornstarch, and flour in a small saucepan and whisk until no lumps remain. Place over medium-high heat and cook, stirring occasionally, until the mixture comes to a boil and becomes very thick. Remove from the heat and add the egg yolk mixture a little at a time. Add the butter and whisk everything to combine, and set aside.

5. Add the remaining sugar to the egg white. Whip, using an electric mixer on high speed, until stiff peaks form.

6. Place the phyllo shells on a baking sheet. Fill equally with the lemon curd. Pipe on the meringue topping to decorate however you wish. Bake for 10 minutes, until lightly golden brown on top. Let cool.

Pro tip:
You will want to make sure these are all eaten on the same day they are made or the bottoms can become soggy. Not that these cuties will last that long!

Cookies and Cream Crispy Bars

Your favorite childhood treat, loaded with sandwich cookies and dipped in white chocolate—oh yes, I went there!

1 tablespoon unsalted butter, plus more for your hands

1 cup mini marshmallows

1 cup crispy rice cereal

½ cup chocolate sandwich cookies, crushed (4 cookies)

½ cup white chocolate chips, melted

1. Place the butter and marshmallows in a large saucepan over medium-low heat. Heat, stirring constantly, until melted.

2. Remove from the heat and add the cereal and cookies. Stir to combine. Pour out the mixture onto a clean work surface. Grease your hands with a small amount of butter and work the mixture into a large bar shape (or whatever shape you wish).

3. Let sit until cooled and set, about 30 minutes. Cut in half and dip the bottom of the bars in the melted white chocolate. Place on a parchment-lined baking sheet and let set.

Variations:

Mix it up! Instead of cookies, add your favorite bite-size candies. Instead of candy or cookies, use dried fruit. Freeze-dried strawberries mixed into the treats and dipped in melted dark chocolate—yum!

Classic Red Velvet Cupcakes

Obsessed with red velvet everything? So am I! But nothing beats the traditional cupcake, right?!

For the cupcakes

2 tablespoons unsalted butter, at room temperature

1 ½ tablespoons granulated sugar

1 ½ tablespoons packed light brown sugar

1 large egg yolk

1 ½ teaspoons red food coloring

½ teaspoon pure vanilla extract

Pinch of salt

¼ teaspoon baking powder

2 tablespoons plus 2 teaspoons sour cream

6 tablespoons all-purpose flour

⅛ teaspoon baking soda

1 tablespoon unsweetened cocoa powder

For the cream cheese frosting

2 ounces cream cheese, softened

2 tablespoons unsalted butter, at room temperature

½ teaspoon vanilla bean paste

1 ¼ cups powdered sugar

Make the cupcakes:

1. Preheat the oven to 350°F. Line three cups of a muffin tin with paper liners.

2. Cream together the butter and sugars in a large bowl, using an electric mixer, for 1 minute. Add the egg yolk, food coloring, and vanilla, mix to combine, then set aside. Mix together the salt, baking powder, sour cream, flour, baking soda, and cocoa powder in a separate bowl. Slowly add the flour mixture to the butter mixture and mix until there are no dry pockets.

3. Divide the batter evenly among the three prepared cups. Bake for 18 to 20 minutes, until a toothpick inserted into the center of a cupcake comes out clean. Remove from the oven and let cool for 5 minutes in the tin, then remove from the tin and let cool completely on a wire rack.

Make the cream cheese frosting:

1. Cream the cream cheese and butter together in a medium bowl, using an electric mixer, until smooth. Add the vanilla and combine. Slowly add the powdered sugar and mix until it is all combined. Beat on high speed for 2 minutes. Frost the cupcakes.

S'mores Dip with Homemade Graham Crackers

An American favorite, the s'more can be enjoyed anytime with this fun alternative recipe! Serve with homemade graham crackers or feel free to enjoy with your preferred cookies, crackers, or fruit!

For the graham crackers

1 cup plus 6 tablespoons whole wheat flour
Pinch of salt
⅛ teaspoon baking soda
⅛ teaspoon ground cinnamon
6 tablespoons unsalted butter, at room temperature
2 tablespoons plus 2 teaspoons granulated sugar
2 tablespoons packed light brown sugar
2 tablespoons honey
½ teaspoon pure vanilla extract
1 large egg yolk
Cooking spray
All-purpose flour for dusting

For the dip

1 cup milk chocolate chips
Large marshmallows

Make the graham crackers:

1. Combine the flour, salt, baking soda, and cinnamon in a medium bowl and stir together; set aside.

2. Place the butter and sugars in a large bowl and cream together, using an electric mixer, for 1 minute. Add the honey, vanilla, and egg yolk and beat to combine. Slowly add the flour mixture and beat until there are no lumps. Refrigerate the mixture, covered, for 1 hour.

3. Preheat the oven to 350°F. Spray a baking sheet with cooking spray. Roll out the dough on a floured work surface to ¼ inch thick. Using a 2-inch square cookie cutter, cut out cookies and place on the prepared baking sheet (you should get 18 to 20 cookies). You can also free cut the cookies to about 2 x 2 inches. Pierce the cookies with a fork to mimic graham crackers.

4. Bake for 10 to 12 minutes, until slightly golden brown along the edges. Let cool completely on a wire rack.

Make the dip:

1. Preheat the oven to 400°F.

2. Place the chocolate chips in a 6-inch oven-safe skillet. Top with the marshmallows in a single layer. Bake for 8 minutes, or to your desired color of marshmallow.

Sauces 'N' Condiments

Green Salsa

1 pound tomatillos, husked
1 poblano pepper
¼ white onion
2 garlic cloves
½ cup loosely packed fresh
   cilantro
½ teaspoon kosher salt
½ teaspoon ground cumin
3 cracks black pepper

1. Preheat the oven to 425°F.

2. Place the oil in a large bowl. Toss the tomatillos, poblano, onion, and garlic in the oil. Transfer to a baking sheet. Roast in the oven for 15 minutes, flipping the items over halfway through. Remove from the oven and let cool completely.

3. Remove the poblano and remove the skin, stem, and seeds. Place the poblano flesh in a blender, add all the remaining ingredients, and blend until smooth.

4. Store in the refrigerator in an airtight container for up to 1 week.

Pickled Red Onions

1 garlic clove, smashed
¼ cup water
½ cup white vinegar
2 tablespoons plus 2 teaspoons
    sugar
1 small red onion, julienned

1. Place all the ingredients, except the onion, in a small saucepan. Heat over medium heat, stirring constantly, until the sugar is dissolved. Remove from the heat, add the onion, and let the pot cool completely on a heat-safe surface.

2. Transfer the mixture to an airtight container and chill in the refrigerator for at least an hour; overnight is best.

3. Store in the refrigerator in an airtight container for up to 2 weeks.

Blue Cheese Dressing

¼ cup mayonnaise
2 tablespoons milk
2 tablespoons sour cream
3½ tablespoons blue cheese
    crumbles
Dash of Worcestershire sauce
¼ teaspoon kosher salt
3 cracks black pepper
2 teaspoons whole-grain
    mustard

1. Whisk together all the ingredients in a small bowl or cup.

2. Chill in the refrigerator for at least 1 hour.

3. Store in the refrigerator in an airtight container for up to 1 week.

Lemon Vinaigrette

1 tablespoon fresh lemon juice
2 tablespoons Rosemary Garlic
    Olive Oil (page 175)
1 teaspoon whole-grain
    mustard
2 teaspoons honey
Pinch of kosher salt
1 crack black pepper

1. Whisk together all the ingredients in a small bowl or cup.

2. Store in the refrigerator in an airtight container for up to 2 weeks.

Garlic Salad Dressing

½ cup mayonnaise
½ teaspoon minced garlic
1 tablespoon distilled white
    vinegar
1 teaspoon sugar
¼ teaspoon paprika
½ teaspoon Worcestershire
    sauce
¼ teaspoon dried oregano
1 teaspoon whole-grain
    mustard
Pinch of kosher salt
2 cracks black pepper

1. Whisk together all the ingredients in a bowl.

2. Store in the refrigerator in an airtight container for up to 2 weeks.

Roasted Garlic

1 head garlic
1 teaspoon olive oil
1 crack black pepper
Pinch of kosher salt

1. Preheat the oven to 375°F.

2. Cut about ¾ inch off the top of the garlic, until the cloves are exposed. Discard the cut pieces of garlic or keep them for other recipes. Place garlic head, otherwise intact, in a piece of foil large enough to wrap it in. Drizzle the olive oil over the exposed cloves, adding the pepper and salt on top. Tightly wrap the garlic in the foil. Bake for 45 minutes to 1 hour. The garlic is done when a toothpick inserted into the largest clove feels no resistance.

3. Place the garlic, still wrapped in foil, on a countertop to cool until completely cool. Using your hands, squeeze the garlic from the bottom on the bulb up, until all the garlic comes out of the cloves.

4. Store in the refrigerator in an airtight container for up to 2 weeks.

Garlic Mayonnaise

6 cloves Roasted Garlic
    (page 174)
½ cup mayonnaise
2 cracks black pepper
Pinch of kosher salt

1. Mash the garlic in a small bowl, using a fork, until it forms a paste.

2. Mix with the other ingredients, cover, and chill in refrigerator.

3. Store in the refrigerator in an airtight container for up to 2 weeks.

Rosemary Garlic Olive Oil

1 cup extra virgin olive oil
3 cloves garlic, peeled and
    smashed
2 fresh rosemary sprigs

1. Place all of the ingredients into a small pan. Let cook over medium low heat for 5 minutes, until fragrant. Let cool completely in the pan. Drain and discard any solids.

2. Store in the refrigerator in an airtight container for up to 1 week.

Cocktail Sauce

1 cup ketchup
1 tablespoon prepared cream-
   style horseradish

1. In small bowl, mix the ingredients together.

2. Cover with plastic wrap and chill in the refrigerator until ready to serve.

3. Store in the refrigerator in an airtight container for up to 2 weeks.

Tartar Sauce

1 cup mayonnaise
⅓ cup dill pickle relish
¼ teaspoon garlic powder
¼ teaspoon onion powder
¼ teaspoon kosher salt
2 cracks black pepper

1. Combine all the ingredients.

2. Cover with plastic wrap, and chill in the refrigerator for at least 1 hour.

3. Store in the refrigerator in an airtight container for up to 2 weeks.

Basil Pesto

MAKES ABOUT ¾ CUP

2 cups packed fresh basil leaves
  (1 ounce)
1 garlic clove, roughly chopped
¼ cup pine nuts
½ cup extra virgin olive oil
½ cup freshly grated
  Parmigiano-Reggiano
Pinch of salt
2 cracks black pepper

1. Place the basil, garlic, pine nuts, and olive oil in a blender and blend until smooth. Add the cheese, salt, and pepper. Mix until combined.

2. Store in the refrigerator in an airtight container for up to 1 week.

Taco Seasoning

MAKES ABOUT
4 TABLESPOONS SEASONING

2 tablespoons all-purpose flour
2 teaspoons ground cumin
1 teaspoon kosher salt
1½ teaspoons chili powder
½ teaspoon paprika
¼ teaspoon garlic powder
¼ teaspoon onion powder
¼ teaspoon dried oregano
⅛ teaspoon chipotle powder

1. Place all the ingredients in a small bowl and whisk to combine.

2. Store in the pantry in an airtight container for up to 1 year.

ACKNOWLEDGMENTS

First of all, I would like to thank the readers and followers of my blog, *This Silly Girl's Kitchen*. There is no way I would have been able to acheive my biggest dream, this cookbook, without your support.

To Jeremy, for putting up with my shenanigans while allowing me to focus 110 percent on *The Cozy Table*. For Starbucks runs, to taste testing and overall believing in me, you are my world! (After food, of course . . . okay, maybe not after food.)

To my parents, Dale and Mike, (1) for bringing me into this world, that was pretty important; and (2) for cheering me along every step of the way. Not only with this book, but life in general. No matter what I would have wanted to be when I "grow up," you would have supported me. But, without your instilling in me when I was young that I could achieve any goal, I would not be where I am today.

To my late Grandma Helen, with whom I was lucky to have a chance to talk about this book. She was the first person who really made me excited about cooking. I will forever have special memories of us elbow deep in dumpling dough in her kitchen.

To my two besties, Cami and Parrish. Your daily advice, reassurance, and laughter helped me to really keep my head up even when times were hard in our blogging world. You are more than just blogging friends; I consider you both my real-life besties.

To my editor and the staff at The Countryman Press. Thank you for believing in my inner twelve-year-old's dream of publishing a cookbook. You all are truly amazing to work with!

And last, but mostly cutely, to Dakota and Peanut for licking up every last delicious crumb from the kitchen floor.

xoxo, Dana

INDEX

For information about permission to reproduce selections from this book, write to
Permissions, The Countryman Press, 500 Fifth Avenue, New York, NY 10110

For information about special discounts for bulk purchases, please contact
W. W. Norton Special Sales at specialsales@wwnorton.com or 800-233-4830

Manufacturing by Versa Press
Book design by Natalie Olsen, Kisscut Design
Production manager: Devon Zahn

The Countryman Press
www.countrymanpress.com

A division of W. W. Norton & Company, Inc.
500 Fifth Avenue, New York, NY 10110
www.wwnorton.com

978-1-68268-092-6

10 9 8 7 6 5 4 3 2 1